GENOCIDE **&** PERSECUTION

The Kurds

Titles in the Genocide and Persecution Series

GENOCIDE & PERSECUTION

I The Kurds

Noah Berlatsky
Book Editor

Frank Chalk
Consulting Editor

GREENHAVEN PRESS
A part of Gale, Cengage Learning

GALE
CENGAGE Learning·

Detroit • New York • San Francisco • New Haven, Conn • Waterville, Maine • London

Elizabeth Des Chenes, *Director, Publishing Solutions*

For more information, contact:
Greenhaven Press
27500 Drake Rd.
Farmington Hills, MI 48331-3535
Or you can visit our Internet site at gale.cengage.com.

For product information and technology assistance, contact us at:

Gale Customer Support, 1-800-877-4253
For permission to use material from this text or product, submit all requests online at www.cengage.com/permissions

Further permissions questions can be emailed to permissionrequest@cengage.com

Every effort is made to ensure that Greenhaven Press accurately reflects the original intent of the authors. Every effort has been made to trace the owners of copyrighted material.

Cover image © Everett Collection Inc./Alamy.
Interior barbed wire artwork © f9photos, used under license from Shutterstock.com.

LIBRARY OF CONGRESS CATALOGING-IN-PUBLICATION DATA

The Kurds / Noah Berlatsky, book editor.
      p. cm. -- (Genocide and persecution)
   Includes bibliographical references and index.
   ISBN 978-0-7377-6257-0 (hardcover)
  1. Kurds--Crimes against--Iraq. 2. Kurds--Crimes against--Turkey. 3. Kurds--Iraq--Politics and government. 4. Kurds--Turkey--Politics and government. 5. Kurdistan--Politics and government. I. Berlatsky, Noah.
   DS70.8.K8K855 2013
   305.891'5970561--dc23

                                                                  2012025470

Printed in the United States of America
1 2 3 4 5 6 7 16 15 14 13 12

Contents

An American reporter argues that Saddam Hussein's policy of repression and relocation against the Kurds is horrific, but says that it does not rise to the level of genocide.

Preface

> *"For the dead and the living, we must*
> *bear witness."*
>
> Elie Wiesel, Nobel laureate and
> Holocaust survivor

The histories of many nations are shaped by horrific events involving torture, violent repression, and systematic mass killings. The inhumanity of such events is difficult to comprehend, yet understanding why such events take place, what impact they have on society, and how they may be prevented in the future is vitally important. The Genocide and Persecution series provides readers with anthologies of previously published materials on acts of genocide, crimes against humanity, and other instances of extreme persecution, with an emphasis on events taking place in the twentieth and twenty-first centuries. The series offers essential historical background on these significant events in modern world history, presents the issues and controversies surrounding the events, and provides first-person narratives from people whose lives were altered by the events. By providing primary sources, as well as analysis of crucial issues, these volumes help develop critical-thinking skills and support global connections. In addition, the series directly addresses curriculum standards focused on informational text and literary nonfiction and explicitly promotes literacy in history and social studies.

Each Genocide and Persecution volume focuses on genocide, crimes against humanity, or severe persecution. Material from a variety of primary and secondary sources presents a multinational perspective on the event. Articles are carefully edited and introduced to provide context for readers. The series includes volumes on significant and widely studied events like the Holocaust, as well as events that are less often studied, such as the East Pakistan genocide in what is now Bangladesh. Some volumes focus on multiple events endured by a specific people, such as the Kurds, or multiple events enacted over time by a particular oppressor or in a particular location, such as the People's Republic of China.

Each volume is organized into three chapters. The first chapter provides readers with general background information and uses primary sources such as testimony from tribunals or international courts, documents or speeches from world leaders, and legislative text. The second chapter presents multinational perspectives on issues and controversies and addresses current implications or long-lasting effects of the event. Viewpoints explore such topics as root causes; outside interventions, if any; the impact on the targeted group and the region; and the contentious issues that arose in the aftermath. The third chapter presents first-person narratives from affected people, including survivors, family members of victims, perpetrators, officials, aid workers, and other witnesses.

In addition, numerous features are included in each volume of Genocide and Persecution:

- An annotated **table of contents** provides a brief summary of each essay in the volume.
- A **foreword** gives important background information on the recognition, definition, and study of genocide in recent history and examines current efforts focused on the prevention of future atrocities.
- A **chronology** offers important dates leading up to, during, and following the event.
- **Primary sources**—including historical newspaper accounts, testimony, and personal narratives—are among the varied selections in the anthology.
- **Illustrations**—including a world map, photographs, charts, graphs, statistics, and tables—are closely tied

to the text and chosen to help readers understand key points or concepts.

- **Sidebars**—including biographies of key figures and overviews of earlier or related historical events—offer additional content.
- **Pedagogical features**—including analytical exercises, writing prompts, and group activities—introduce each chapter and help reinforce the material. These features promote proficiency in writing, speaking, and listening skills and literacy in history and social studies.
- A **glossary** defines key terms, as needed.
- An annotated list of international **organizations to contact** presents sources of additional information on the volume topic.
- A **list of primary source documents** provides an annotated list of reports, treaties, resolutions, and judicial decisions related to the volume topic.
- A **for further research** section offers a bibliography of books, periodical articles, and Internet sources and an annotated section of other items such as films and websites.
- A comprehensive subject **index** provides access to key people, places, events, and subjects cited in the text.

The Genocide and Persecution series illuminates atrocities that cannot and should not be forgotten. By delving deeply into these events from a variety of perspectives, students and other readers are provided with the information they need to think critically about the past and its implications for the future.

Foreword

The term *genocide* often appears in news stories and other literature. It is not widely known, however, that the core meaning of the term comes from a legal definition, and the concept became part of international criminal law only in 1951 when the United Nations Convention on the Prevention and Punishment of the Crime of Genocide came into force. The word *genocide* appeared in print for the first time in 1944 when Raphael Lemkin, a Polish Jewish refugee from Adolf Hitler's World War II invasion of Eastern Europe, invented the term and explored its meaning in his pioneering book *Axis Rule in Occupied Europe*.

Humanity's Recognition of Genocide and Persecution

Lemkin understood that throughout the history of the human race there have always been leaders who thought they could solve their problems not only through victory in war, but also by destroying entire national, ethnic, racial, or religious groups. Such annihilations of entire groups, in Lemkin's view, deprive the world of the very cultural diversity and richness in languages, traditions, values, and practices that distinguish the human race from all other life on earth. Genocide is not only unjust, it threatens the very existence and progress of human civilization, in Lemkin's eyes.

Looking to the past, Lemkin understood that the prevailing coarseness and brutality of earlier human societies and the lower value placed on human life obscured the existence of genocide. Sacrifice and exploitation, as well as torture and public execution, had been common at different times in history. Looking toward a more humane future, Lemkin asserted the need to punish— and when possible prevent—a crime for which there had been no name until he invented it.

Legal Definitions of Genocide

On December 9, 1948, the United Nations adopted its Convention on the Prevention and Punishment of the Crime of Genocide (UNGC). Under Article II, genocide

> means any of the following acts committed with intent to destroy, in whole or in part, a national, ethnical, racial or religious group, as such:
>
> (a) Killing members of the group;
>
> (b) Causing serious bodily or mental harm to members of the group;
>
> (c) Deliberately inflicting on the group conditions of life calculated to bring about its physical destruction in whole or in part;
>
> (d) Imposing measures intended to prevent births within the group;
>
> (e) Forcibly transferring children of the group to another group.

Article III of the convention defines the elements of the crime of genocide, making punishable:

> (a) Genocide;
>
> (b) Conspiracy to commit genocide;
>
> (c) Direct and public incitement to commit genocide;
>
> (d) Attempt to commit genocide;
>
> (e) Complicity in genocide.

After intense debate, the architects of the convention excluded acts committed with intent to destroy social, political, and economic groups from the definition of genocide. Thus, attempts to destroy whole social classes—the physically and mentally challenged, and homosexuals, for example—are not acts of genocide under the terms of the UNGC. These groups achieved a belated but very significant measure of protection under international criminal law in the Rome Statute of the International Criminal

Court, adopted at a conference on July 17, 1998, and entered into force on July 1, 2002.

The Rome Statute defined a crime against humanity in the following way:

any of the following acts when committed as part of a widespread and systematic attack directed against any civilian population:

(a) Murder;

(b) Extermination;

(c) Enslavement;

(d) Deportation or forcible transfer of population;

(e) Imprisonment or other severe deprivation of physical liberty in violation of fundamental rules of international law;

(f) Torture;

(g) Rape, sexual slavery, enforced prostitution, forced pregnancy, enforced sterilization, or any other form of sexual violence of comparable gravity;

(h) Persecution against any identifiable group or collectivity on political, racial, national, ethnic, cultural, religious, gender . . . or other grounds that are universally recognized as impermissible under international law, in connection with any act referred to in this paragraph or any crime within the jurisdiction of this Court;

(i) Enforced disappearance of persons;

(j) The crime of apartheid;

(k) Other inhumane acts of a similar character intentionally causing great suffering, or serious injury to body or to mental or physical health.

Although genocide is often ranked as "the crime of crimes," in practice prosecutors find it much easier to convict perpetrators of crimes against humanity rather than genocide under domestic laws. However, while Article I of the UNGC declares that countries adhering to the UNGC recognize genocide as "a crime under international law which they undertake to prevent and to punish," the Rome Statute provides no comparable international mechanism for the prosecution of crimes against humanity. A treaty would help individual countries and international institutions introduce measures to prevent crimes against humanity, as well as open more avenues to the domestic and international prosecution of war criminals.

The Evolving Laws of Genocide

In the aftermath of the serious crimes committed against civilians in the former Yugoslavia since 1991 and the Rwanda genocide of 1994, the United Nations Security Council created special international courts to bring the alleged perpetrators of these events to justice. While the UNGC stands as the standard definition of genocide in law, the new courts contributed significantly to today's nuanced meaning of genocide, crimes against humanity, ethnic cleansing, and serious war crimes in international criminal law.

Also helping to shape contemporary interpretations of such mass atrocity crimes are the special and mixed courts for Sierra Leone, Cambodia, Lebanon, and Iraq, which may be the last of their type in light of the creation of the International Criminal Court (ICC), with its broad jurisdiction over mass atrocity crimes in all countries that adhere to the Rome Statute of the ICC. The Yugoslavia and Rwanda tribunals have already clarified the law of genocide, ruling that rape can be prosecuted as a weapon in committing genocide, evidence of intent can be absent when convicting low-level perpetrators of genocide, and public incitement to commit genocide is a crime even if genocide does not immediately follow the incitement.

Several current controversies about genocide are worth noting and will require more research in the future:

1. Dictators accused of committing genocide or persecution may hold onto power more tightly for fear of becoming

vulnerable to prosecution after they step down. Therefore, do threats of international indictments of these alleged perpetrators actually delay transfers of power to more representative rulers, thereby causing needless suffering?

2. Would the large sum of money spent for international retributive justice be better spent on projects directly benefiting the survivors of genocide and persecution?

3. Can international courts render justice impartially or do they deliver only "victors' justice," that is the application of one set of rules to judge the vanquished and a different and laxer set of rules to judge the victors?

It is important to recognize that the law of genocide is constantly evolving, and scholars searching for the roots and early warning signs of genocide may prefer to use their own definitions of genocide in their work. While the UNGC stands as the standard definition of genocide in law, the debate over its interpretation and application will never end. The ultimate measure of the value of any definition of genocide is its utility for identifying the roots of genocide and preventing future genocides.

Motives for Genocide and Early Warning Signs

When identifying past cases of genocide, many scholars work with some version of the typology of motives published in 1990 by historian Frank Chalk and sociologist Kurt Jonassohn in their book *The History and Sociology of Genocide*. The authors identify the following four motives and acknowledge that they may overlap, or several lesser motives might also drive a perpetrator:

1. To eliminate a real or potential threat, as in Imperial Rome's decision to annihilate Carthage in 146 BC.

2. To spread terror among real or potential enemies, as in Genghis Khan's destruction of city-states and people who rebelled against the Mongols in the thirteenth century.

3. To acquire economic wealth, as in the case of the Massachusetts Puritans' annihilation of the native Pequot people in 1637.
4. To implement a belief, theory, or an ideology, as in the case of Germany's decision under Hitler and the Nazis to destroy completely the Jewish people of Europe from 1941 to 1945.

Although these motives represent differing goals, they share common early warning signs of genocide. A good example of genocide in recent times that could have been prevented through close attention to early warning signs was the genocide of 1994 inflicted on the people labeled as "Tutsi" in Rwanda. Between 1959 and 1963, the predominantly Hutu political parties in power stigmatized all Tutsi as members of a hostile racial group, violently forcing their leaders and many civilians into exile in neighboring countries through a series of assassinations and massacres. Despite systematic exclusion of Tutsi from service in the military, government security agencies, and public service, as well as systematic discrimination against them in higher education, hundreds of thousands of Tutsi did remain behind in Rwanda. Government-issued cards identified each Rwandan as Hutu or Tutsi.

A generation later, some Tutsi raised in refugee camps in Uganda and elsewhere joined together, first organizing politically and then militarily, to reclaim a place in their homeland. When the predominantly Tutsi Rwanda Patriotic Front invaded Rwanda from Uganda in October 1990, extremist Hutu political parties demonized all of Rwanda's Tutsi as traitors, ratcheting up hate propaganda through radio broadcasts on government-run Radio Rwanda and privately owned radio station RTLM. Within the print media, *Kangura* and other publications used vicious cartoons to further demonize Tutsi and to stigmatize any Hutu who dared advocate bringing Tutsi into the government. Massacres of dozens and later hundreds of Tutsi sprang up even as Rwandans prepared to elect a coalition government led by moderate political parties, and as the United Nations dispatched a small international military force led by Canadian general Roméo Dallaire to oversee the elections and political transition. Late in 1992, an international human rights organization's investigating team detected the hate propaganda campaign, verified systematic massacres of Tutsi, and warned the international community that Rwanda had already entered the early stages of genocide, to no avail. On April 6, 1994, Rwanda's genocidal killing accelerated at an alarming pace when someone shot down the airplane flying Rwandan president Juvenal Habyarimana home from peace talks in Arusha, Tanzania.

Hundreds of thousands of Tutsi civilians—including children, women, and the elderly—died horrible deaths because the world ignored the early warning signs of the genocide and refused to act. Prominent among those early warning signs were: 1) systematic, government-decreed discrimination against the Tutsi as members of a supposed racial group; 2) government-issued identity cards labeling every Tutsi as a member of a racial group; 3) hate propaganda casting all Tutsi as subversives and traitors; 4) organized assassinations and massacres targeting Tutsi; and 5) indoctrination of militias and special military units to believe that all Tutsi posed a genocidal threat to the existence of Hutu and would enslave Hutu if they ever again became the rulers of Rwanda.

Genocide Prevention and the Responsibility to Protect

The shock waves emanating from the Rwanda genocide forced world leaders at least to acknowledge in principle that the national sovereignty of offending nations cannot trump the responsibility of those governments to prevent the infliction of mass atrocities on their own people. When governments violate that obligation, the member states of the United Nations have a responsibility to get involved. Such involvement can take the form of, first, offering to help the local government change its ways

through technical advice and development aid, and second—
if the local government persists in assaulting its own people—
initiating armed intervention to protect the civilians at risk. In
2005 the United Nations began to implement the Responsibility
to Protect initiative, a framework of principles to guide the international community in preventing mass atrocities.

As in many real-world domains, theory and practice often
diverge. Genocide and crimes against humanity are rooted in
problems that produce failing states: poverty, poor education,
extreme nationalism, lawlessness, dictatorship, and corruption.
Implementing the principles of the Responsibility to Protect doc-
trine burdens intervening state leaders with the necessity of ad-
dressing each of those problems over a long period of time. And
when those problems prove too intractable and complex to solve
easily, the citizens of the intervening nations may lose patience,
voting out the leader who initiated the intervention. Arguments
based solely on humanitarian principles fail to overcome such
concerns. What is needed to persuade political leaders to stop
preventable mass atrocities are compelling arguments based on
their own national interests.

Preventable mass atrocities threaten the national interests of
all states in five specific ways:

1. Mass atrocities create conditions that engender widespread and concrete threats from terrorism, piracy, and
   other forms of lawlessness on the land and sea;
2. Mass atrocities facilitate the spread of warlordism, whose
   tentacles block affordable access to vital raw materials
   produced in the affected country and threaten the prosperity of all nations that depend on the consumption of
   these resources;
3. Mass atrocities trigger cascades of refugees and internally
   displaced populations that, combined with climate change
   and growing international air travel, will accelerate the
   worldwide incidence of lethal infectious diseases;

4. Mass atrocities spawn single-interest parties and political agendas that drown out more diverse political discourse in the countries where the atrocities take place and in the countries that host large numbers of refugees. Xenophobia and nationalist backlashes are the predictable consequences of government indifference to mass atrocities elsewhere that could have been prevented through early actions;

5. Mass atrocities foster the spread of national and transnational criminal networks trafficking in drugs, women, arms, contraband, and laundered money.

Alerting elected political representatives to the consequences of mass atrocities should be part of every student movement's agenda in the twenty-first century. Adam Smith, the great political economist and author of *The Wealth of Nations*, put it best when he wrote: "It is not from the benevolence of the butcher, the brewer, or the baker that we expect our dinner, but from their regard to their own interest." Self-interest is a powerful engine for good in the marketplace and can be an equally powerful motive and source of inspiration for state action to prevent genocide and mass persecution. In today's new global village, the lives we save may be our own.

Frank Chalk

Frank Chalk, who has a doctorate from the University of Wisconsin-Madison, is a professor of history and director of the Montreal Institute for Genocide and Human Rights Studies at Concordia University in Montreal, Canada. He is coauthor, with Kurt

Jonassohn, of The History and Sociology of Genocide *(1990); coauthor with General Roméo Dallaire, Kyle Matthews, Carla Barqueiro, and Simon Doyle of* Mobilizing the Will to Intervene: Leadership to Prevent Mass Atrocities *(2010); and associate editor of the three-volume Macmillan Reference USA* Encyclopedia of Genocide and Crimes Against Humanity *(2004). Chalk served as president of the International Association of Genocide Scholars from June 1999 to June 2001. His current research focuses on the use of radio and television broadcasting in the incitement and prevention of genocide, and domestic laws on genocide. For more information on genocide and examples of the experiences of people displaced by genocide and other human rights violations, interested readers can consult the websites of the Montreal Institute for Genocide and Human Rights Studies (http://migs.concordia.ca) and the Montreal Life Stories project (www.lifestoriesmontreal.ca).*

World Map

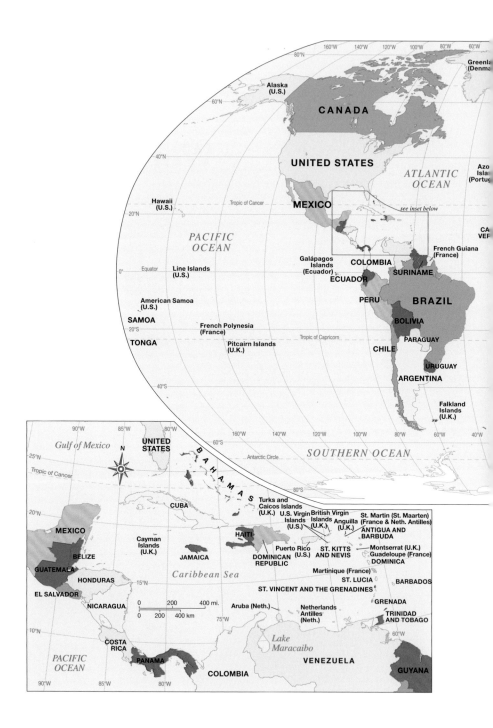

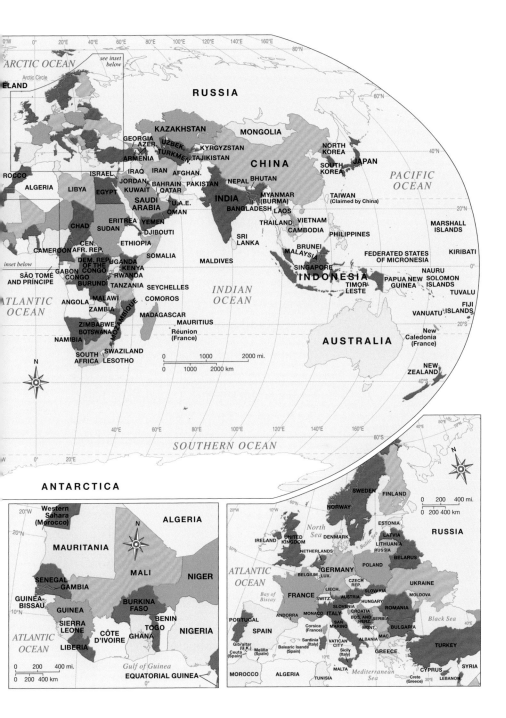

ARCTIC OCEAN

see inset below

Arctic Circle

ELAND

RUSSIA

60°N

KAZAKHSTAN

MONGOLIA

GEORGIA
AZER. UZBEK. KYRGYZSTAN
ARMENIA TURKMEN. TAJIKISTAN

NORTH
KOREA

JAPAN

40°N

ROCCO

SOUTH
KOREA

CHINA

ISRAEL IRAQ IRAN AFGHAN.

NEPAL BHUTAN

TAIWAN
(Claimed by China)

ALGERIA LIBYA EGYPT

JORDAN BAHRAIN PAKISTAN
KUWAIT QATAR

PACIFIC
OCEAN

SAUDI
ARABIA

U.A.E.
OMAN

INDIA

MYANMAR
(BURMA) LAOS

BANGLADESH

20°N

MARSHALL
ISLANDS

CHAD

ERITREA YEMEN
SUDAN DJIBOUTI

THAILAND VIETNAM
CAMBODIA

SRI
LANKA

PHILIPPINES

CAMEROON CEN.
AFR. REP.

ETHIOPIA

SOMALIA

MALDIVES

BRUNEI
MALAYSIA

FEDERATED STATES
OF MICRONESIA

KIRIBATI

inset below

DEM. REP. UGANDA
OF THE KENYA
GABON CONGO
CONGO RWANDA
BURUNDI

SINGAPORE

NAURU

0°

SÃO TOMÉ
AND PRÍNCIPE

INDONESIA

PAPUA NEW SOLOMON
GUINEA ISLANDS

ATLANTIC
OCEAN

TANZANIA SEYCHELLES

INDIAN
OCEAN

TIMOR-
LESTE

TUVALU

ANGOLA

MALAWI
ZAMBIA

COMOROS

MADAGASCAR

VANUATU

FIJI
ISLANDS

20°S

ZIMBABWE
BOTSWANA

MOZAMBIQUE

MAURITIUS

Réunion
(France)

New
Caledonia
(France)

AUSTRALIA

NAMIBIA

SWAZILAND

SOUTH LESOTHO
AFRICA

0   1000   2000 mi.

0   1000   2000 km

N

NEW
ZEALAND

40°S

40°E   60°E   80°E   100°E   120°E   140°E   160°E

60°S

SOUTHERN OCEAN

W   0°   20°E

ANTARCTICA

20°W Western
Sahara
(Morocco)

ALGERIA

20°N

MAURITANIA

N

MALI

NIGER

SENEGAL
GAMBIA

BURKINA
FASO

GUINEA-
BISSAU

GUINEA

BENIN

SIERRA
LEONE

CÔTE TOGO
D'IVOIRE GHANA

NIGERIA

ATLANTIC
OCEAN

LIBERIA

0   200   400 mi.

0   200   400 km

Gulf of Guinea

EQUATORIAL GUINEA

0°

SWEDEN FINLAND

0   200   400 mi.

0   200 400 km

NORWAY

ESTONIA

North
Sea DENMARK

RUSSIA

IRELAND UNITED
KINGDOM

LATVIA
LITHUANIA
RUSSIA

NETHERLANDS

BELARUS

ATLANTIC
OCEAN

BELGIUM
LUX.

GERMANY

POLAND

Bay of
Biscay

FRANCE

LIECH.
SWITZ. AUSTRIA

CZECH
REP.

SLOVAKIA

UKRAINE

HUNGARY

MOLDOVA

ANDORRA

MONACO ITALY

SLOVENIA
CROATIA

ROMANIA

PORTUGAL

SAN
MARINO

BOS. AND SERBIA
HERZ.

SPAIN

Corsica
(France)

VATICAN
CITY

MONT.

BULGARIA

Black Sea

40°N

Gibraltar
(U.K.)
Ceuta
(Spain)

Melilla
(Spain)

Sardinia
(Italy)

Balearic Isands
(Spain)

Sicily
(Italy)

MAC.
ALBANIA

GREECE

TURKEY

CYPRUS

SYRIA

MALTA

Mediterranean
Sea

Crete
(Greece)

LEBANON

MOROCCO   ALGERIA   TUNISIA

17

Chronology

1915–1918	The Ottoman Empire undertakes a genocide against ethnic Armenians. In many cases Kurds help in the extermination of the Armenians.
1958	The Iraqi monarchy is overthrown. A new Iraqi constitution recognizes Kurdish rights.
1961	Kurds rebel in northern Iraq.
March 1970	The Iraqi government and Kurdish parties agree to a peace treaty that grants Kurds autonomy.
March 1974	Disputes over oil rights and other issues causes Mullah Mustafa Barzani, the leader of the Kurdish Democratic Party (KDP), to declare a rebellion against the Iraqi government. Iran provides aid for the Kurds.
March 1975	Iran withdraws aid and the rebellion disintegrates.
June 1975	A new Kurdish party, the Patriotic Union of Kurdistan (PUK), splits from the KDP.
1978	Violence erupts between the KDP and the PUK in Iraq.
1980	The Iran-Iraq war begins.
1982	Turkey adopts a new constitution; critics say it discriminates against Kurds.

1984	In Turkey, the PKK (Kurdistan Workers' Party) launches a guerilla war to achieve a separate Kurdish state.
1988	Iraq launches the Anfal campaign against Kurds, who have been supporting Iran in the war. Tens of thousands of Kurdish civilians are killed.
March 16, 1988	Iraq launches a poison gas attack on the Kurdish town of Halabja.
August 2, 1990	Iraq invades neighboring Kuwait over a border dispute.
January 17, 1991	A US-led and UN-sanctioned coalition invades Iraq to force it to leave Kuwait. Iraqi troops are soon forced to leave Kuwait.
March 1991	Following the Iraqi defeat, Kurds rise up hoping to attain independence. US forces refuse to aid the rebellion, and it is put down, forcing hundreds of thousands of Kurds to flee into the mountains.
April 1991	US forces create a safe haven for Kurdish refugees. Kurdish leaders negotiate with Saddam Hussein for Kurdish autonomy.
1992	Turkish troops cross the Iraqi border to attack PKK safe havens in Iraq.
May 1994	Civil war breaks out between the PUK and the KDP for control of the semiautonomous Kurdish region in Iraq.
1995	Turkey launches a major military operation against Kurds in northern Iraq.

September 1998	A peace treaty is signed between the PUK and the KDP.
August 2002	As part of its bid for European Union membership, Turkey lifts bans on Kurdish education and broadcasting.
March 20, 2003	US-led coalition forces invade Iraq, claiming that Saddam Hussein is concealing weapons of mass destruction. Kurdish fighters aid US forces against Saddam Hussein's regime.
April 9, 2003	US forces take central Baghdad.
June 2004	In Turkey, state TV broadcasts its first Kurdish-language program.
January 2005	A Kurdish party alliance comes in second in Iraq's historic post-Saddam elections.
April 2005	PUK leader Jalai Talabani is elected interim Iraqi president by its parliament.
June 2005	The first session of Kurdish Parliament is held in the Kurdish autonomous region. Massoud Barzani is named president.
December 2007	Turkey launches air strikes on Kurdish rebel bases in Iraq. It later sends in ground troops.
October 2011	PKK rebels kill twenty-four Turkish troops near the Iraqi border. Turkey and Iran agree to cooperate against Kurdish militants.

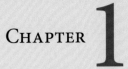

CHAPTER 1

Historical Background on the Kurds

Chapter Exercises

STATISTICS

	Iraq	Turkey
Total Area	438,317 sq km World ranking: 59	783,562 sq km World ranking: 37
Population	31,129,225 World ranking: 39	79,749,461 World ranking: 17
Ethnic Groups	Arab 75–80%; Kurdish 15–20%; Turkoman, Assyrian, or other 5%	Turkish 70–75%; Kurdish 18%; other minorities 7–12%
Religions	Muslim 97% (Shia 60-65%, Sunni 32–37%); Christians or other 3%	Muslim 99.8% (mostly Sunni); Other .2% (mostly Christians and Jews)
Literacy (total population)	74.1%	87.4%
GDP	$127.2 billion World ranking: 62	$1.053 trillion World ranking: 17

Source: *The World Factbook*. Washington, DC: Central Intelligence Agency, 2012. www.cia.gov.

1. Analyzing Statistics

Question 1: There are many more Kurds living in Turkey than there are living in Iraq. Does this mean that Kurds are a larger percentage of the population in Turkey than in Iraq? Explain your answer referring to the statistics above.

Question 2: Based on the Kurds' experience in Iraq and Turkey, which do you think is more important in determining whether a minority is oppressed, its total numbers or its percentage of the population? Explain your answer.

Question 3: Look at the ethnic and religious breakdowns in both Iraq and Turkey. Which factor do you think has been most important in the oppression of the Kurds in these countries, religion or ethnicity? Explain your answer.

2. Writing Prompt

Write an article describing the 1988 use of chemical weapons by Saddam Hussein against the Kurds. Begin the article with a strong title that will capture your audience. Include any appropriate background to help a reader better understand the event. Be sure to include details about who, what, when, where, and why.

3. Group Activity

In small groups, discuss whether you believe that the Kurds should be granted an independent homeland made up of parts of Iraq, Turkey, Syria, and Iran. Write a speech recommending the action that you believe the United Nations should take and explain your reasoning.

An Overview of the Kurds

Amir Hassanpour

In the following viewpoint, a Kurdish scholar says that the Kurds are the world's largest ethnic group without a state. He explains that the Kurdistan region has been the site of ethnic conflict and atrocities since before the modern era. Modern nation-states have continued the tradition of persecution; Turkey, Iraq, Iran, Syria, and other nations in the region have all launched genocidal and targeted ethnic violence against the Kurds. He says that this violence continues today, and that more needs to be done to end it. Amir Hassanpour is a prominent Iranian Kurdish scholar and associate professor in the Department of Near and Middle Eastern Civilizations at the University of Toronto.

The Kurds are often referred to as the world's largest non-state nation. The population is estimated at between 25 to 35 million, which makes them the fourth-largest ethnic group in the Middle East, outnumbered only by Arabs, Turks, and Persians. The majority live in Kurdistan, a borderless homeland whose territory is divided among the neighboring countries of Turkey, Iran, Iraq, and Syria. Some Kurdish populations are scattered throughout western and central Asia and, since the 1960s, can also be found in Europe, North America, Australia, New Zealand, and other countries.

Ancient Kurdistan

The territory's rich natural resources have supported nomadic populations practicing animal husbandry, as well as rural and urban economies rooted in agriculture, long-distance trade, and regional markets. According to historical and archeological evidence, the region was the site of the world's earliest agrarian societies, cities, and states, all of which coexisted uneasily in a web of antagonisms that were rooted in cleavages based on class, empire, ethnicity, religion, race, and gender.

Although the Kurds appear to be an indigenous people of Western Asia, living largely astride the Zagros Mountains, their territory was home to numerous other civilizations and peoples, as well. Most of these (except for Assyrians, Armenians, and Jews) are now extinct or have been assimilated into the Kurdish population. The landscape is full of relics of monumental construction projects ranging from ancient irrigation networks to bridges and citadels, side by side with evidence of the ongoing destruction of life and property through conquest, wars, massacres, and forced population movements.

Pre-Modern States

We have more knowledge about the Kurds in the years following the conquest of the region by Islamic armies in the seventh century. Kurdistan lay very close to Baghdad, the capital of the Islamic caliphate. It was the site of incessant wars among the armies of the caliphs, as well as governors, Kurdish rulers, and conquerors coming from as far as the Roman empire in the west and Mongolia in the east. Although the conflicts were primarily over land, taxes, and the recruitment of military service from the population, ethnic and religious differences also provided justifications for conquest and subjugation. Unrestrained violence, including atrocities against both civilians and combatants was widespread, and was aimed, in part, at intimidating the adversary and the population into submission. To give one example, the army of Adhud al-Dawla, ruler of the Buwayhid dynasty centered in Baghdad, besieged the Hakkari Kurds in 980, forced them into surrender on a promise of sparing their lives, but then crucified them and left their bodies hanging along 15 miles of roadside near Mosul.

Several factors helped to reshape the ethnic composition of Western Asia. For one, the Oghuz Turks arrived in the region from the Asian steppes in the eleventh century. Also important was the formation of the Seljuk dynasty (11th through 13th centuries) and Turkoman dynasties (Aq Qoyunlu and Qara Qoyunlu), which were followed by the fall of the caliphate in 1258 in the wake of the Mongol invasion. According to historian Vladimir Minorsky, "the Kurdish element was exhausting itself" in these unceasing wars. It is during this period, however, that the Kurds emerge as a distinct people, their territory becomes identified by outsiders as Kurdistan, and Kurdish statehood emerges in the form of mini-states and principalities.

Some of the indigenous populations of Kurdistan include the Armenians, Assyrians (Christians), and Kurds (mostly Muslims). There are also other groups, such as the Yezidis, who are followers of minority religions, as well as scattered minorities such as the Jews. These peoples survived the intensive colonization of the region by Turkic (Oghuz, Turkoman, Ottoman) and Mongol nomadic and tribal peoples from central Asia. The homogenizing force of centuries of conversion, forcible population movements, and massacres was offset by the inability of feudal states to centralize power and therefore assimilate their conquered peoples of the region into the language, culture and religion of the conquerors. Equally important in preventing the total annihilation of the indigenous populations was the labor-intensive nature of feudal agrarian production. Without a sizeable productive labor force, the fertile lands of Armenia, Azerbaijan,

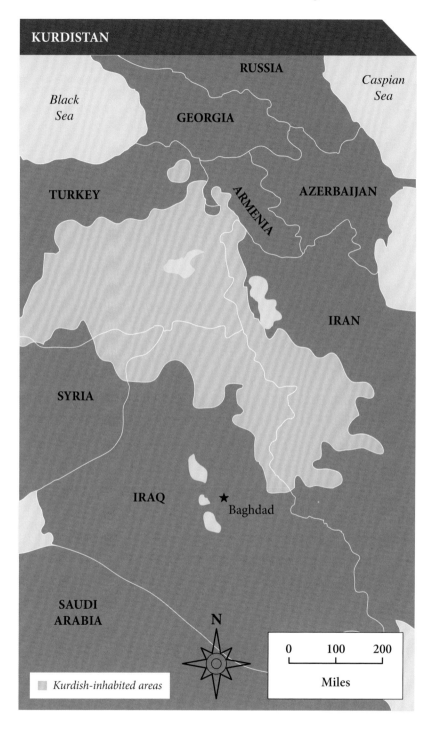

KURDISTAN

RUSSIA

Caspian
Sea

Black
Sea

GEORGIA

TURKEY

ARMENIA

AZERBAIJAN

IRAN

SYRIA

IRAQ

★ Baghdad

SAUDI
ARABIA

N

| 0 | 100 | 200 |

Miles

Kurdish-inhabited areas

Kurdistan, and Mesopotamia could not sustain elaborate state structures. Although some Kurdish territories were Turkicized due to conquest and the violent elimination of Kurdish ruling families (especially by the Aq Qoyunlu dynasty, 1378–1508), as well as by massacres and deportations, some Kurdish mini-states were, nonetheless, gaining ground.

By the early sixteenth century, Western Asia was under the rule of two rival Turkish dynasties, the Ottomans and Safavids, which in 1639 drew their borders along the Zagros mountain range. Armenia and Kurdistan were thus divided, and the region experienced intermittent wars. The two empires pursued a policy of administrative centralization by removing hereditary Kurdish principalities. However, the Kurdish mini-states benefitted from the rivalry between the dynasties, and some survived until the mid-nineteenth century. Shah Abbas I (1588–1626) was suspicious of the loyalty of the Kurdish rulers of the principalities of Biradost and Mukriyan. He supervised and personally participated in the massacres of the rulers and their subjects (1610–1611), and resettled Turkish tribes in their territory. He deported another 15,000 Kurds from another region of Kurdistan to northeastern Iran. An eyewitness to the mass killings, the Shah's official chronicler Eskandar Monshi Torkman, whose *History of Shah Abbas the Great* was translated into English in 1971, detailed with pride the "general massacre" of the Mukri Kurds and noted that the shah's "fury and wrath" could not be allayed "but by shedding the blood of those unfortunate ones" and that the "slicing of men" and the "enslavement of women and girls . . . had been inscribed on the annals of time by destination." He labeled the Kurds as "base-born," "human beings of savage disposition," and "impious."

The Modern Nation-State

In the mid-nineteenth century, Ottoman Turkey and Iran began adopting a more European style of administrative and military centralization. The two states used their armies to overthrow the six remaining Kurdish principalities, and extended their direct rule over all parts of Kurdistan. With the emergence of modern style nation-states in Iran (after the Constitutional Revolution of 1906 to 1911) and Ottoman Turkey (especially after the 1908 Young Turk revolution), the Kurds were incorporated into the state as citizens rather than a distinct people enjoying the right to self-rule. Feudal and tribal relations continued to prevail in the predominantly rural society of Kurdistan, but Kurdish nationalist ideas began to appear in the poetry and journalism of the last decade of the nineteenth century.

World War I turned Kurdistan into a battlefield between the Ottomans, Russians, Iranians, and British. The Ottoman government committed genocide against Armenians and Assyrians in 1915, and forcibly transferred some 700,000 Kurds to Western Turkey in 1917. At the same time, the tsarist Russian army conducted massacres of the Kurds in Sauj Bulagh in 1915 (now Mahabad, Iran), Rawandiz (Iraq), Khanaqin (Iran), and throughout the eastern parts of Kurdistan. As in previous wars, both armies committed crimes against humanity, including enslavement, murder, extermination, rape, sexual slavery, sexual violence, and persecution. They also engaged in such war crimes as willful killing, inhuman treatment, unlawful deportation and transfer, attacking civilians, pillaging, and cruel treatment. The Russian army also committed gendercide—the killing of adolescent and adult males—in the massacre of Sauj Bulagh, and carried away some 400 women and girls for abuse. Armenian and Assyrian militias participated in the Russian massacres, and some Kurdish tribal, feudal, and religious leaders acted as accomplices in the genocide of Armenians and Assyrians. At the same time, many Kurds sheltered Armenian victims, and Assyrians helped starving Kurds.

The dismantling of the Ottoman empire in World War I led to the division of its Kurdish region and the incorporation of that territory into the newly created states of Iraq (under British occupation and mandate, 1918–1932), Syria (under French occupation and mandate, 1918–1946), and Turkey (Republic of Turkey since 1923). The formation of these modern nation-states entailed the forced assimilation of the Kurds into the official or dominant national languages and cultures: Turkish (Turkey), Persian (Iran), and Arabic (Syria, and, in a more limited scope, Iraq). In Turkey and Iran, in particular, the political power of religious, tribal, and feudal leaders was uprooted. State violence was the principal means of integration and assimilation. According to historian Mark Levene, (Ottoman) Turkey had turned Eastern Anatolia, which includes Armenia and Kurdistan, into a "zone of genocide" from 1878 to 1923. This "zone" has persisted into the twenty-first century.

Kurdish resistance to assimilation was diverse and extensive, including a series of armed revolts in Turkey (1921, 1925, 1927–1931, 1937–1938), Iran (1920–early 1930s), and Iraq (early 1920s, 1940s). These revolts were led, often jointly, by heads of religious orders (*sheikhs*) and feudal and tribal chiefs (*aghast*) as well as an emerging group of nationalist intelligentsia, political activists, and deserting army officers, who were mostly urban and secular. The repression of these revolts was most brutal in Turkey and Iran.

The region was not a theater of war in World War II, except for the northern part of Iranian Kurdistan, which was occupied by the Soviet Union from 1941 to 1946. After the war the four countries acceded or ratified the 1949 Geneva Conventions [which regulate the conduct of warfare] (Turkey, 1954; Iran, 1957; Iraq, 1956; Syria, 1953) and its 1977 Additional Protocols.

Turkey

The intent to commit genocide is inscribed, explicitly, in Turkey's Law No. 2510 of 1934, which stipulated the transfer of non-Turks to Turkish speaking regions, where they would not be allowed to form more than 5 percent of the population. This law provided for the depopulation of non-Turkish villages and towns, resettlement of Turks in non-Turkish areas, and other assimilationist projects, such as the establishing of boarding schools, which were intended to turn non-Turkish children into monolingual Turkish speakers. The law was applied a year later in the wake of Law No. 2884, which decreed the systematic Turkification of the Dersim region, renamed as Tunceli, through military control, boarding schools, the banning of the Kurdish language and culture, changing place names, and deportation.

This forced Turkification project led to the Dersim uprising, which the army and the air force brutally suppressed from 1937 to 1938, and the repression of which some researchers consider to be an act of genocide. The Turkish Republic considered popular uprisings to be reactionary and religious opposition to the civilizing and westernizing policies of the Turkish nation-state. The Kurds were branded as tribal, uncivilized, illiterate, primitive, backward, dirty, and ignorant. Any expression of Kurdish identity was treated as a crime against the "indivisibility of the Turkish nation" and "territorial integrity" of Turkey.

Dersim was the last uprising until the armed resistance of 1984–1999, led by the Kurdistan Workers Party (PKK, in Kurdish acronyms). Nonetheless, various governments continued Turkification through the deliberate elimination of Kurdish as a spoken and written language, and through ethnocide—eliminating Kurdish culture and ethnic identity. The use of the Kurdish language, music, dance, dress, personal and geographic names, and even listening to broadcasting and recorded music were all criminalized by the Turkish state.

Because of Turkey's aspirations to full membership in the European Union, the parliament acceded to pressure and legalized the private use of spoken Kurdish in 1991. A decade later the parliament removed some of the constitutional and legal restrictions on the language. However, linguistic genocide continues to be the official state policy.

During its repression of the PKK, which it labeled counterinsurgency operations, Turkey declared a state of emergency in parts of its southeastern (Kurdish) territory. According to

A group of Kurdish rebels stands in the ruins of a village in northern Iraq in 1963. The rebels sought to create an independent state. © Bettmann/Corbis.

the Human Rights Watch, Turkey committed "gross violation of its international commitments to respect the laws of war" (1995). This included forced displacements, indiscriminate shootings, summary executions, and disguising the identity of perpetrators, as well as violations of international law, including summary execution, torture, forcible displacement of civilians, pillage, destruction of villages, failure to care for civilians displaced by government forces, injury of civilians, destruction of civilian property, inhumane and degrading treatment, kidnaping of civilians to act as porters and as human shields against attack, disappearances, life-threatening conditions of detention, and inadequate medical attention leading to death. The Human Rights Watch also noted that the United States, Turkey's close ally and its major weapons supplier, was deeply implicated, and, much like NATO, chose to "downplay Turkish violations for strategic reasons." It also charged that the PKK, which was not party to the Geneva Protocols, also engaged in "substantial violations of the laws of war," including "summary executions, indiscriminate fire and the intentional targeting of non-combatants."

During the operations, according to a Turkish parliamentary commission, the armed forces displaced 378,335 villagers while destroying or evacuating 3,428 rural settlements (905 villages and 2,523 hamlets) from the mid-1980s to 1997. These figures are generally treated as underestimations. The Turkish security forces further destroyed the infrastructure of rural life in the Kurdish region, and thus threatened the survival of the Kurds as a distinct people. Other crimes included systematic sexual violence against women in custody.

Iran

Especially under Reza Shah Pahlavi (1925–1941), Iran undertook a policy of forcible Persianization of the Kurds through linguicide and ethnocide as well as war, killing, jail, and deportations. As early as 1923, speaking Kurdish had been banned in schools and other state institutions, and by the mid-1930s, a total ban on the language and culture was imposed. Under the Pahlavi dynasty (1925–1979), crimes against humanity and war crimes were committed in military operations against the Kurds. The Islamic regime that followed the Shahs continued the Persianization policy, although on a more limited scale. During its suppression of Kurdish autonomists, which began once it came to power, the government committed crimes against humanity including murder, extermination, imprisonment, and torture, and war crimes such as willful killing, inhuman treatment, appropriation of property, denying a fair trial, unlawful deportation and transfer, attacking civilians, execution without due process, and attacking undefended places.

Iraq

Iraq was the only country, other than the Soviet Union, where the existence of the Kurds was recognized and the Kurdish language was allowed limited use in primary education, local administration, and the mass media. However, Iraq did institute a policy of containing Kurdish nationalism through Arabization. The government committed crimes against humanity and war crimes during the long conflict with Kurdish autonomists, which raged intermittently from 1961 to the 1990s. During the first Ba'ath regime's offensive against the Kurds in 1963, the Mongolian People's Republic asked the UN General Assembly to discuss "the policy of genocide carried out by the government of the Republic of Iraq against the Kurdish people," and the Soviet Union referred the case to the Economic and Social Council. Mongolia later withdrew the request, and the Economic and Social Security Council refused to consider the Soviet request.

The second Ba'ath regime (1968–2003) constructed a cordon sanitaire [that is, a quarantine line] along its northern borders with Iran and Turkey by destroying hundreds of Kurdish villages soon after the defeat of the Kurdish armed resistance in 1975. In 1983 it killed all the adolescent and adult males of Barzani Kurds, numbering about 8,000. In addition, during its war with Iran (1980–1988), in violation of the 1925 Geneva Protocol, the regime used chemical weapons against both the Iranians and Iraqi Kurds who lived in a number of settlements, including the town of Halabja (March 16, 1988). Moreover, the oil-rich Kirkuk region was Arabized by forcibly uprooting Kurds from the city and villages. The 1988 campaign of mass murder, code-named Operation *Anfal* ("spoils" of war, also the title of a chapter in the Koran), is widely considered a genocide. According to a 1993 report by the Human Rights Watch, it entailed the killing of more than 100,000 Kurds, the disappearance of tens of thousands of noncombatants, the destruction of 4,006 villages (according to Kurdistan Regional Government), the forced displacement of hundreds of thousands of villagers, the arbitrary arrest and jailing of thousands of women, children, and the elderly under conditions of extreme deprivation, and the destruction of rural life.

Syria
Although the Kurds of Syria have not engaged in armed conflict with the state, they were targeted for ethnic cleansing beginning in the early 1960s. Some 120,000 Kurds were stripped of Syrian citizenship. According to a 1991 report by the Middle East Watch, the Syrian government planned for the depopulation of Kurdish regions by creating an "Arab belt" along the Turkish border, evicting peasants from 332 villages, and replacing them with Arab settlers.

Soviet Union and Caucasia
Although the Kurdish communities of Soviet Caucasia and Turkmenistan enjoyed cultural and linguistic rights, thousands of Caucasian Kurds were subjected to two waves of forced deportation to the Central Asian republics of Kazakhstan, Kirgizia, and Uzbekistan in 1937 and 1944. During the disintegration of the Soviet Union, the Muslim Kurdish populations of Armenia and Nagorny-Karabakh were largely displaced in the course of the war between Armenia and Azerbaijan between 1990 and 1994, when, according to the Human Rights Watch, both countries "systematically violated the most basic rule of international humanitarian law."

Prevention, Education, and Political-Judicial Reform

Since ancient times, mass killing and related crimes have been a permanent feature of life in the region. Modern genocide in Kurdistan is distinguished from earlier crimes by its rootedness in the nation-state and its nationalist ideology, which safeguards the territorial integrity of the homeland.

While there is little progress in reversing state politics, citizens, both Kurds and non-Kurds, have taken significant steps toward recognizing, documenting, and resisting genocide in literary words, academic research, conferences, film, and journalism. Much remains to be done, however, toward legal-political reform, promoting genocide education, and monitoring early warning signs of impending crimes.

Turkey's 1934 Settlement Law Targets Non-Turks Including Kurds

Erol Ülker

In the following viewpoint, a scholar on Turkish history says that the 1934 Turkish settlement law was based on a rising sense of Turkish nationalism and on a conviction that Turkey should be united by Turkish language and ethnicity. It stated that Muslim immigrants who did not speak Turkish should have been assimilated by the government, according to the writer. He says that the law also gave the Turkish authorities the power to settle or resettle those inside Turkey based on the government's perception of their Turkishness. Erol Ülker is a PhD candidate at the University of Chicago.

In June 1932, a bill concerning the adoption of a new Settlement Law was forwarded to the Turkish Grand National Assembly. This was certainly not the first time that a law on settlement was on the agenda, for the Turkish Parliament had already issued a number of official decrees, directives and laws for regulating the immigration-settlement policies since the promulgation of the Republic in 1923. Moreover, there was already a specific law on settlement in effect when this bill came to the parliamentary

Erol Ülker, "Assimilation, Security and Geographical Nationalization in Interwar Turkey: The Settlement Law of 1934," *European Journal of Turkish Studies*, 2008. Copyright © 2008 by European Journal of Turkish Studies. All rights reserved. Reproduced by permission.

discussions, Settlement Law 885, adopted in 1926. Yet the drafters of the law proposal made it clear that something broader was intended. They emphasized the assimilative design of the new law [which would come to be known as Law 2510] by bringing up the need for measures to promote the use of Turkish by those who remained removed from 'Turkish culture'. The provisions of the new law were expected to furnish these measures.

Assimilation and the Settlement Law

The deputies repeated the same assimilative concerns with the drafters of the law proposal in the parliamentary discussions preceding the adoption of the new law in 1934. Sadri Maksudi, a deputy of the Republican People Party, for example, stated that:

> Turkification of the language is among the greatest devices for assuring the future of the Turkish race and the living of Turk as Turk. This is our aim.

Şükrü Kaya, Minister of Interior of the time, expressed the intention of the government in the most lucid way possible, saying:

> This law will create a country speaking with one language, thinking in the same way and sharing the same sentiment.

The use of such terms as race, descent and blood in the law proposal and the deputies' speeches in the Grand National Assembly was clearly inspired by the prevailing Turkish nationalist discourse which became increasingly characterized by open ethno-cultural references in the political context of the 1930s. This tendency . . . [was] based on the understanding that all Turks constituted a 'super-family' that could be distinguished from others through its ethnic and genealogical characteristics.

Language and Culture

The phrasing of Law 2510 was under the influence of this context as well. Terms like 'the Turkish race' and 'descent' appeared prominently in the final draft of the law, echoing the prevailing nationalist ideology of the period. Yet 'Turkish culture' was the most critical concept of the Settlement Law. It was clearly associated with speaking Turkish as one's native tongue. This becomes clear in the documents that regulated the admission of immigrants and their naturalization into Turkish citizenship. A circular issued by the General Directorate of Settlement in order to govern the application of Law 2510 specified who were eligible for immigration as:

> individuals of Turkish race or individuals connected to Turkish culture who speak Turkish and who do not know any other language.

Moreover, a person of 'Turkish culture' was officially considered to be a Muslim individual who spoke no other language but Turkish. This left all the non-Muslim communities, along with the non-Turkish-speaking Muslims, beyond the official margins of Turkish culture:

> Foreign Kurds, Arabs, Albanians; other Muslims who speak languages other than Turkish and all foreign Christians and Jews cannot be given nationality declaration documents. And they cannot be given immigrant paper. They all will be treated as foreigners.

The ruling elite privileged, however, certain Muslim communities that were not necessarily Turkish speakers. As far as the status of immigration rights to Turkey was concerned, Pomaks, Bosnians, Tatars and Karapapaks were supposed to be treated in the same way with the individuals of Turkish culture. Furthermore,

> Muslim Georgian, Lezgi, Chechen, Circassian, Abkhazian and other Muslims who are deemed to be connected to Turkish culture will be assigned nationality declaration documents with the order of the center.

It should be emphasized at this point that these groups were not defined as peoples of Turkish culture, but they were supposed to be treated as such. This nuance made it possible for, say, a Bulgarian-speaking Pomak to immigrate to Turkey. S/he was supposed to be regarded as being of Turkish culture, i.e. a Turkish-speaking Muslim, even if s/he spoke Bulgarian as a native language. Yet this contradiction was to have been overcome with the assimilation of this hypothetical Pomak into Turkish culture by learning Turkish and forgetting Bulgarian.

Law 2510 furnished the administration with a set of measures to assimilate not only the members of such immigrant communities, but also thousands of other Muslims that still did not speak Turkish as a mother tongue ten years after the establishment of the Republic, as well as a large nomadic population throughout the country. In this respect, the first article of Law 2510 gave the right to the Ministry of Interior to govern the distribution of the population across the country on the basis of adherence to Turkish culture. Article 11 comprised very important measures, which were deployed, according to the drafters of the law, to assure 'unity in language, culture and blood'. It charged the Ministry of Interior with preventing the foundation of villages and districts by non-Turkish speakers. The Ministry also employed specific measures against those who did not possess Turkish culture or did not speak Turkish though 'possessing Turkish culture'. These measures consisted of population transfers aiming to disperse such people within the country and depriving them of citizenship when necessary.

Zones of Settlement

The most striking stipulation of Law 2510 was the second article under the rubric of 'Settlement Regions'. It divided the country into three settlement zones in which the conditions for settling were strictly tied to the individual's relationship to Turkish culture.

Type One Zones: Places where the concentrating of populations of Turkish culture is desired.

Type Two Zones: Places set aside for the relocation and settlement of populations whose assimilation into Turkish culture is desired.

Type Three Zones: Places that will be uninhabited, and where settlement and residence will be prohibited due to spatial, sanitary, cultural, political, military and security reasons.

A number of additional provisions regulated the conditions of inhabitance of the settlement zones in a detailed manner. These provisions seem to have been concerned with nationalizing the population inhabiting Type One Zones. Type Two Zones, on the other hand, were chosen as appropriate regions for the assimilation of the targeted groups.

Paragraph Four of Article 10 gave the Ministry of Interior the authority to transfer nomads or settled tribesmen not possessing Turkish culture to Type Two Zones. According to Article 12, the non-Turkish speakers who inhabited Type One Zones and were not transferred to Type Two Zones ought to be settled in the centers of villages, districts and provinces whose populations were of Turkish culture. The same article prohibited the settlement of new tribesmen, nomads and others who did not possess Turkish culture in Type One Zones.

The Kurds Hoped for Equality and Peace on the Eve of Iraq's Independence

Ibrahim Ahmad

In the following speech delivered after the successful Iraqi revolution of 1958, a Kurdish intellectual and political leader details Kurdish oppression at the hands of both Western imperialists and the Iraqi monarchy. This oppression included discrimination and efforts to suppress the Kurdish language. He says that Kurds have fought with Arabs to overthrow that monarchy, which is linked to Western nations. He maintains that Kurds are prepared to be enthusiastic citizens of the new Iraqi republic, and urges the republic to recognize Kurds as equals with Arabs. Ibrahim Ahmad was the general secretary of the Iraqi Kurdish Democratic Party (KDP).

A glance at Kurdish–Arab relations ever since the Kurds became Muslims clearly demonstrates that the two neighboring peoples have continued to co-exist on the basis of friendly, peaceful, and cooperative ties. In the Islamic era, the grounds for these ties were the Islamic principles which call for equality among all Muslims and state that there is no difference between an Arab and a non-Arab except in piety and good deed. Under Ottoman [Turkish] rule, both peoples experienced much op-

Ibrahim Ahmad, "Speech of July 27, 1958," *Mustafa Barzani and the Kurdish Liberation Movement*, edited by Ahmed Ferhadi. New York: Palgrave Macmillan, 2003, pp. 175–177.

pression and injustice, hunger and hardship from a common enemy who turned the land into a supply depot and the people into a military encampment to provide for their endless wars. After the First World War [ending in 1918], the victorious imperialist countries [Britain, France, and the United States] partitioned the lands of Arabs and Kurds among themselves as plunder. After the truce was proclaimed, Britain occupied what was called the Mosul Vilayet, of which the vast majority of the inhabitants are Kurds. This led to what is known as the Mosul Question, which was then resolved by a plebiscite [a direct vote of the people] in which some of the Kurds who took part voted in favor of forming a Kurdish state and others voted in favor of coexistence with the Arabs, provided they enjoyed a measure of decentralized administration. Thereafter, the Mosul Vilayet, including southern Kurdistan, was officially annexed to Iraq in 1926.

Discrimination Against the Kurds

Because the old Iraqi Constitution was promulgated prior to the annexation, it contained nothing pertaining to the national rights of the Kurds. This special administration favored by those Kurds who wanted to live within Iraq was limited to guaranteeing the rights of the Kurds in speeches delivered on ceremonial occasions by the British and Iraqi officials, to some promises Britain made at the League of Nations [the predecessor of the United Nations] in 1932, and to the "Local Languages Act" [of 1931, which provided some recognition of the Kurdish language]. However, despite the trivial nature of these rights, the British and the few Iraqi rulers who took their cues from them did not allow the Kurds to enjoy them. During the long years of monarchic rule, the Kurds were subjected to oppression of two kinds. First, they shared with the Iraqi people poverty, ignorance, disease, and heavy-handed tyranny; second, they underwent ethnic discrimination and deprivation of national rights.

These conditions bred the Kurdish revolts of which you know, and which imperialists their agents at times described as separatist, British-instigated, or the other extreme, as a Communist movement. At no time were they anything other than a national liberation movement with the goal of rescuing the country from imperialists and their treasonous agents, and recasting Arab–Kurdish ties on a stronger basis for both peoples without interference from the imperialists applying their "divide and rule" axiom. The imperialists knew better than anyone that these revolutions were not separatist because the Kurds know that cessation is detrimental to their cause and enfeebles their position just as much [as] it harms the cause of the Arab people and enfeebles their position. Knowing better than anybody else that these revolutions were not of their making, the imperialists brutally and forcefully suppressed them and provided all they could to their Iraqi lackeys to maintain this suppression. What would Britain gain by instigating the Kurds against their obedient minions who provided conditions they never even imagined to satisfy their greedy, imperialistic cravings? If these movements were supported by the imperialists, why did they not succeed?

After all, weren't the imperialists responsible for partitioning the Kurdish homeland? The imperialists and their stooges knew that these movements were not Communist because the economic, social, and political development of the Kurdish people was not at the level to become a Communist movement. They made these unjust assertions in order to justify their vicious attacks on the Kurdish revolution and to distort their reputation, misdirecting Arab anger against the Kurds in accordance with their imperialistic "divide and rule" policy. Not only did the Kurds rise up on their own behalf but they also took part in every Iraqi liberation movement as well. For this, they suffered imprisonment, deportation, forced exile and killings over and above the mass killings, deportations, and exiles which they suffered because of their own revolts; the most hideous example of which was done to the valorous Barzan tribe and their beautiful country because they engaged in a liberation movement against repressive imperialism, corrupt conditions, and the decadent

Rebel soldiers pose in Baghdad, Iraq, in July 1958 by a pedestal that reads "long live leader of revolution Kassem and his heroic brothers." Kurds and Arabs fought together to overthrow the Iraqi monarchy. © AP Images.

ruling clique. The ruling clique under the monarchy resorted to other means to fight these movements in addition to its criminal suppression of the movements of the Kurdish people. First, it joined the Sa'ad Abad Accord, then it signed the Turco–Iraqi Agreement of 1946, and finally it joined the Baghdad Pact.

A Double Struggle

Among the objectives of these pacts and agreements was the tightening of the noose around the Kurdish liberation movement from every side and collectively finishing it off. Another objective was to hinder Kurdish progress by applying an oppressive racist policy, of which the following are only a few examples:

Excerpts from the 1970 Iraqi Constitution and 1974 Autonomy Law Guaranteeing Kurdish Rights

Constitution of Iraq (1970) (exerpts: Articles 5, 8(c))

Article 5

(a) Iraq is part of the Arab nation;

(b) The Iraqi people consists of two main ethnic groups: Arabs and Kurds. This Constitution recognizes the ethnic rights of the Kurdish people, as well as the legitimate rights of all minorities, within the framework of Iraqi unity.

Article 8(c)

The region in which the majority of the population are Kurds shall enjoy autonomy in accordance with the provisions of the law.

Summary of Act No. 33 of 11 March 1974 (as amended through 1983)

1. The Legal Status of the Autonomous Region

262. Article 1 of Act No. 33 of 1974 stipulates that:

The region of Kurdistan shall enjoy autonomy and shall be regarded as a separate administrative unit endowed with distinct personality within the framework of the legal, political and economic unity of the Republic of Iraq. The region shall be an inseparable part of the territory of Iraq and its people shall constitute an integral part of the Iraqi people. The city of Arbil shall be the headquarters of the autonomous administration and the autonomous institutions shall form part of the institutions of the Republic of Iraq.

263. Under Revolutionary Command Council decision 119 of 4 August 1981, the autonomous institutions referred to in the Autonomy Act report directly to the Council of Ministers. This is a clear indication of the legal importance attached to those autonomous institutions.

2. The Official Language and the Language of Education in the Autonomous Region

264. Article 2 of the above-mentioned Act stipulates that:

(a) In addition to Arabic, Kurdish shall be an official language in the region;

(b) Arabic and Kurdish shall be the languages of education, at all stages and in all establishments, for Kurds in the region, in accordance with paragraph (e) of this article;

(c) Educational facilities for members of the Arab ethnic group shall be established in the region. In such facilities, instruction shall be in Arabic and the Kurdish language shall be taught as a compulsory subject;

(d) All residents of the region, regardless of their mother tongue, shall have the right to choose the schools in which they wish to be taught;

(e) All stages of education in the region shall be governed by the general education policy of the State.

265. Act No. 28 of 1983 stipulated that Arabic and Kurdish would be the languages of instruction for Kurds in the region and that the Arabic language would be taught from the fourth primary grade and at all subsequent stages of education.

3. The Rights of Citizens, whether Arabs or Members of Minority Groups

266. Article 3 of the Act stipulates that:

(a) The rights and freedoms of Arabs and members of minority groups in the region shall be safeguarded in accordance with the provisions of the Constitution . . .

(b) Arabs and members of minority groups in the region shall be represented in all the autonomous institutions on the basis of their number in proportion to the total population of the region . . . .

Hurst Hannum, ed., Documents on Autonomy and Minority Rights. *Boston: Martinus Nighoff, 1993, pp. 317–318.*

First, the embracing appeasement of a small group of Kurdish traitors and renegades and neglect of the Kurdish people. Second, the attempt to wipe out the Kurdish language by not using it as an official language in government offices and by not applying the Local Languages Act except in a few places, and by obstructing and limiting its applications. Third, the reference to Kurdistan as the North and Kurds as the Northerners on all occasions. Fourth, the granting of only a few scholarships to Kurdish students to study abroad and admitting fewer Kurds into Iraqi colleges and universities, without regard to the Kurdish percentage of the total Iraqi population. This resulted in a paucity of educated Kurds to occupy government positions. Fifth, the application of a policy of ethnic discrimination in hiring for government jobs. Sixth, the application of a policy of discrimination in promotions to certain army ranks and the restriction of admission into the Staff Military Academy to a very small number of Kurds. Seventh, the provision of no opportunity to the Kurds to exercise any political rights, even to put out a Kurdish political paper, irrespective of complexion or tendency.

This deliberately wrong, racist policy resulted in keeping the Kurds backward. The Kurds under the monarchy were under a double oppression. Therefore, they struggled to achieve two goals: one, to liberate Iraq from imperialism and the corrupt regime, and the other, to achieve and secure their national rights.

Kurds and Arabs Together

Free Kurds struggled hand in hand with free Arabs in all fields and in all battles. They were imprisoned, killed, or exiled with all their hopes and faith that putting a stop to imperialism and its agents would be enough to prepare the ground for the strongest of ties between the Arab and Kurdish nationalities on the foundations of brotherhood and equality that were predominant in their long history together. Free Kurds fully believed that a victory achieved by the Kurdish people in their liberation struggle was a victory for Arab nationalism in general, and that putting a stop to imperialism and its agents in Iraq was a victory for the cause of both Kurdish and Arab peoples in particular.

Accordingly, and with this faith, the Kurds participated in the blessed revolution [of 1958 against an Iraqi monarchy associated with the British] carried out by the Iraqi army in solidarity with the Iraqi people to end the reign of the corrupt tyrannical gang.

On these grounds and with this faith, they are prepared to defend their fledgling freedom with their blood and souls. The recognition of the Kurdish national rights by the Provisional Constitution and its consideration of Kurd[s] and Arab[s] [as] partners in this homeland are the fruit of our joint struggle and confirm the belief of the free Kurds and free Arabs that the struggle of peoples is an interconnected movement. We look forward to this happy inauguration of the new republican era and we hope that new necessary laws will be legislated to implement the Constitutional guarantee. We hope and believe that steps by our nascent republic to enhance ties with the liberated Arab countries will inevitably be accompanied by a gradual broadening of the Kurdish national rights. Thus, any step taken by the Arab people toward its goals will be a step simultaneously moving the Kurdish people closer to its goals. [If we did that,] we would seal every crevice and fissure in the face of the imperialists and their agents and set an example to be followed for the co-existence of two fraternal peoples under a democratic free system.

While I extend the utmost appreciation of the Kurdish people who are represented by delegations here for the statement in our Provisional Constitution, I wish to express the sincerest of feelings from the Kurdish people toward the nascent [Iraqi] Republic, its free leaders, and brave army. The Kurds are ready to defend their Republic and the national rights they have won with their life's blood, their wealth, and their very souls. Long live the Iraqi Republic, the republic of Arabs and Kurds.

Turkey's Kurds Feel Frustrated and Bitter

Marvine Howe

In the following viewpoint, a journalist reports on unrest and dissatisfaction among Kurds in the Turkish Far East in the early 1980s. She explains that the region suffers from high rates of unemployment, in addition to other challenges. Many Kurds, she says, want independence from Turkey, while others want to escape from the region. The Turkish government, she reports, argues that there is no Kurdish problem, that all ethnicities are treated equally, and that the main need of the region is economic development. Marvine Howe is a former correspondent for the New York Times *and the author of* Morocco: The Islamist Awakening and Other Challenges.

Diyarbakir, Turkey, June 8—People in Turkey's Far East feel neglected. Some want a change of government, others dream of independence and many just want to get out.

Unemployment

The major problem in this predominantly Kurdish area is unemployment; all day and every day the teahouses are full of young men and boys with nothing to do.

Although there is no apparent spillover of the Kurdish revolt in neighboring Iran, there are newly painted independence slogans on walls all over this ancient city on the Tigris, and the level of violence has increased notably in recent months.

In the mainly Kurdish city of Van to the east, four civil servants were caught today putting up posters calling for an independent Kurdistan, and one of them was arrested.

Turkish officials insist there is no "Kurdish problem," maintaining there are no Kurds, only Turks, living in Turkey.

A Secret Struggle Continues

Nevertheless, a Government delegation visited southeast Turkey this week and reported progress in the struggle against "illegal organizations" accused of causing people to flee the region. This is official terminology for clandestine Kurdish groups, said to number about 10.

An extensive tour of the Diyarbakir region and conversations with many people in towns and villages revealed a strong sense of Kurdish identity coupled with deep resentment against the central Government for failing to develop the area while pumping investments into the more prosperous western part of Turkey.

Suggestions for solutions to the problem were mixed, ranging from the demands of extreme separatists to the views of those who say independence is economically unfeasible and instead demand a better deal from Ankara [Turkey's capital].

In the poor quarters of this provincial capital, where streets are unpaved and houses are made of mud brick and wooden poles, slogans on walls in Turkish and Kurdish call for "Freedom for Kurdistan."

Visitors are taken aback by the aggressiveness with which a cafe waiter or gas station attendant declares: "I am Kurdish, not Turk."

"Do you know where you are, in what capital?" a student says in accosting a visitor in the official tourist department. "This is Diyarbakir, capital of Kurdistan."

Turkey vs. the PKK

The Turkish government has instituted certain policies restricting the freedom of the Kurds. For instance, until 2012, minority languages, such as Kurdish, could not be taught in schools. Also, a political party must get 10 percent of the national vote to secure a seat in parliament. It is debated whether this policy aims to assimilate minorities into the majority Turkish culture or to prevent acculturated groups from separating along ethnic lines.

Restrictions such as these alienated the Kurds and resulted in decades of tension between the minority group and the Turkish government. In 1984, the PKK (Kurdistan Workers' Party) declared a Kurdish uprising in an effort to establish an independent Kurdish state. Conflict with Turkish security forces continued until 1999, when the PKK unilaterally declared a cease-fire. The PKK ended its cease-fire in 2004, and the conflict has continued to the present (2012). The Turkish government considers the PKK a terrorist organization.

In its efforts to defeat the PKK, the Turkish government's security forces forced villagers from their homes and sometimes burned villages to the ground. The security forces focused especially on villagers who did not become part of the village guard system and gave food and shelter to members of the PKK. Turkish security forces have also been criticized by Amnesty International for using torture while interrogating PKK members and suspected sympathizers. The PKK in turn targeted villagers who became part of the village guard system and cooperated with the national government. The PKK would often kill the whole family of suspected collaborators.

Underground Kurdish organizations have become active in the last year, according to a professor who asked not to be identified. He said the separatists were centered mainly in high schools and universities. He said they still were a small minority but were gaining influence.

The cease-fire of 1999 ended in 2004 partly because of accusations by Kurds that the Turkish government was not negotiating with them and was still taking action against their forces. The Turkish government blamed the Kurds for attacks on Turkey from Iraqi Kurdistan.

Since the end of the cease-fire, the Turkish government has enacted a number of anti-terrorism laws. In 2005, Article 301 of the Turkish Penal Code, which made it illegal to insult Turkishness, was ratified. The law was amended in 2008 to criminalize an insult to "the Turkish nation." An existing anti-terrorism law was revised in 2006 to define terrorism, among other things, as any act that would weaken or seize the authority of the state, or damage the internal and external security of the state, by means of pressure, force and violence, terror, intimidation, oppression, or threat. In 2007, the Law on Powers and Duties of Police was amended to give police more power to take preventive measures against criminal acts.

These anti-terrorism laws led to a marked increased in the number of human right violations. Security forces have often killed a person for failing to heed a warning to stop, and investigations and prosecutions of these killings have been rare and protracted. In addition, torture methods that leave no physical mark have been used on detainees, according to human rights activists. Often torture is used to extract a confession—despite a legal prohibition against the use of such evidence—and prosecutors have often failed to investigate allegations of torture.

The Turkish government has placed the total number of casualties as a result of conflicts between the Turks and the PKK at approximately 44,000 between 1984 and 2008. Of these casualties, approximately 32,000 were PKK members, 6,500 were soldiers, and 5,500 were civilians. More than 1,500 casualties were reported for the period between 2008 and 2011.

This source said much of the recent violence here, officially attributed to right-left conflicts or family feuds, was the work of these secret organizations. In one incident, three policemen were killed. The professor predicted a Kurdish explosion within a year or two if the situation was not brought under control.

"We want democracy, not independence," said a teacher in Kahta, 90 miles southwest of here. The teacher complained about a total lack of industry in the city of more than 20,000. He said his family and friends favored former Prime Minister Bulent Ecevit, who was "the poor man's leader."

Region Is Quiet Despite Killings

There was little interest shown here in the troubles in the Kurdish areas in neighboring countries. Even a border incident a week ago in which 10 Turkish peasants were killed by Iraqi troops did not provoke a strong reaction.

The Kurds are a fairly homogenous Moslem tribal society of Indo-European origin, living largely in inaccessible mountain regions of southeastern Turkey, western Iran and northern Iraq and Syria. Nobody knows how many Kurds there are, but they are believed to number well over 10 million with perhaps 5 million in Turkey.

Kurdish secessionist movements have appeared periodically in Iraq and Iran in recent years and Kurds have made some gains toward local autonomy in Iraq, but there has been no serious Kurdish revolt in Turkey since insurrections in the 1920's and 1930's. There has been sporadic Kurdish unrest here, but progress has been made toward assimilation through education, migration to western industrial areas and participation in national democratic institutions. It is estimated that about 80 people of Kurdish origin are sitting in the 635-member Turkish Parliament.

"I don't accept a Kurdish problem; the population of Turkey is all Turks, all equal under the law," said the Governor of Diyarbakir, Erdogan Sahinoglu. He stressed in an interview that Turkey was "not concerned" about troubles in the neighboring countries of Iran, Syria and Iraq.

The Governor said that anarchy was a national problem and that things were relatively calm here. He conceded there were some "illegal organizations," made up mostly of young boys who went around painting "kurtulus," or "independence," on the city walls. But he emphasized that this was not a serious problem.

Diyarbakir's main problems are economic, according to the Governor, who was appointed by the Demirel Government when it came to power six months ago. He pointed out that there were only three factories here, making textiles, milk and cheese, and raki, the traditional Turkish spirits. He said construction was under way on a cigarette plant and a wine factory but said his main hope for the future laid in the Karakaya dam, scheduled for completion by 1986.

A well-to-do landowner here, who complained that most of the rich people had left the area for Istanbul or the United States, said the only solution to problems in Diyarbakir and elsewhere in the country was for the two main parties, the governing conservative Justice Party and the opposition Republican Peoples Party, to work together.

The chief of the opposition Republican Peoples Party, Hasan Deger, said that Kurdish unrest was not a big problem and that the crucial need was economic development.

"We don't believe in racialism," Mr. Deger said. "We're all the same people, Kurds, Turks." He was in fact critical of Diyarbakir's elected Mayor, Mehdi Zana, for allegedly favoring Kurds for municipal jobs.

Saddam Hussein Is Accused of Using Poison Gas Against the Kurds

Al Gore

In the following viewpoint, then-US senator Al Gore contends that Saddam Hussein, the leader of Iraq, is perpetrating genocide against the Kurds. He says that Iraq's genocidal policies include the use of chemical weapons—that is, poisonous gas. He argues that the United States must take steps to prevent the atrocities committed against the Kurds. He suggests talking to Iraq's trading partners and with the Soviet Union to encourage them to condemn Iraq. He also maintains the United States should speak out against Iraq, and should issue reports exposing its genocidal policies. Al Gore was a Democratic senator from Tennessee before becoming US vice president in 1993; he is currently an author and environmental activist.

M r. President [that is, the president pro tempore, the person presiding over the Senate], according to extensive and apparently well-documented reports, the Government of Iraq may right now be in the midst of trying to impose a final solution on its Kurdish population. Upward of 100,000 Kurds have already

Al Gore, "Iraq's Use of Chemical Weapons," *The Kurdish Question in US Foreign Policy: A Documentary Sourcebook*, edited by Lokman I. Meho. Westport, CT: Greenwood Publishing, 2004, pp. 57–58. Copyright © 2004 by ABC-CLIO, LLC, Santa Barbara, CA. All rights reserved. Reproduced by permission.

fled the Iraqi Army by crossing over the border into Turkey. Something on the order of 50,000 Kurds remain trapped inside a forbidden zone said to have been marked by the Government of Iraq for depopulation. These people are now the object of a military program, which, according to many reports, includes the use of chemical weapons.

The United States Must Act

If the world does not respond to these developments, we may again be forced to look on as yet another act of mass atrocity is committed by yet another government whose behavior will yet again stain the honor of humanity and of civilization. At such times, there can be no such thing as innocent bystanders. For governments to have knowledge of such events, and not to cry out, is to become complicit with them.

Last week, the United States finally broke the silence, cynicism and indifference which, until then, typified the world's response to repeated charges of inhumane behavior by Iraqi forces, involving the use of chemical weapons. The Secretary of State [James Baker]—convinced by information at his disposal— bluntly laid it on the line for Iraq. Thanks to Senator [Claiborne] Pell [Democrat from Rhode Island], the Senate did likewise, by approving legislation aimed at cutting off United States aid to Iraq, and ending United States imports of Iraqi oil.

It is a beginning, but it is not enough. To achieve results, we should focus world opinion on a demand that Iraq desist from the use of chemical weapons; that it allow international inspection to follow up on claims that chemical weapons have been used; and that it conform its behavior toward the Kurdish population within its borders to norms acceptable under the U.N. Charter and international law.

Actions to Take

To that end, Mr. President, there are certain actions I urgently recommend:

A Kurd woman sits on a makeshift hospital bed in Oshnavieh, Iran, after fleeing a chemical gas attack in August 1988. Thousands were killed by Iraqi chemical weapons attacks on Kurd villages. © Getty Images.

First, our Government should immediately issue a statement which presents the evidence against Iraq in the fullest possible detail.

Second, we should request an immediate session of the Security Council to address the charge that Iraq is in the process of carrying out a genocidal policy.

Third, we should call upon our allies, some of whom are deeply involved with Iraq as trading partners and/or military suppliers, to demand that Iraq be responsive to these charges.

Fourth, we should directly confront the nations of the neutral-nonaligned movement with their silence in the face of the evidence and demand that they speak out.

Fifth, we should ask the Soviet Union to speak out in the same manner as have we. Parallel United States and Soviet approaches will do more than anything else to signal Iraq's leaders that they must change course.

Sixth, we should communicate with every nation that is a party to the Geneva Protocol on the Prohibition of the Use of Chemical Weapons, to advise that silence in the presence of such a challenge to this agreement will make it a dead letter.

Seventh, we should move speedily to determine the needs of Kurdish refugees in Turkey, and of agencies seeking to aid them, including both the United Nations and the Government of Turkey itself. We should make sure that these needs are met.

What the Senate Can Do

To promote these actions, Mr. President, there are certain steps which we in this body can take.

First, the Senate should call upon the Secretary of State to provide public testimony as to the nature of information at his disposal, and as to the administration's ongoing plans.

Second, I suggest that both parties through their leaders consider setting up a clearinghouse process to collect and analyze information on behalf of the Senate as a whole.

Third, we can communicate with the Turkish Government through its ambassador here, to express appreciation for what it has done so far to provide refuge for Kurdish refugees, and to indicate that the Senate is ready to respond to their material needs for our part in this process.

Fourth, we can communicate with the Soviet Government through its ambassador here, urging them to join the United States in public condemnation of Iraqi behavior.

Fifth, we can and should communicate with governments of Iraq's trading partners, suppliers, and supporters; appealing to them to speak out and to use their influence.

Sixth, we can and should make sure that the American people are alerted to what is going on. To this end, we can use not only our own resources, but we ought to ask the two Presidential candidates [Republican George H.W. Bush and Democrat Michael Dukakis] to speak out.

Mr. President, ruthless as it may be, the Government of Iraq is not irrational. Its leaders are aware of world opinion, and understand that their vital interests can be damaged by a hardening of that opinion against them. Recognizing this, we can influence the outcome of these events. But only if we shake world opinion awake.

The Kurds Rebel in Iraq and Turkey After the Gulf War

John Yemma

In the following viewpoint, a US newspaper reports that Kurds are attempting to organize a rebellion against Saddam Hussein in Iraq after the end of the Gulf War, in which the United States defeated Iraq after Iraq invaded Kuwait. The article explains that the rebellion is hindered by the fact that other nations in the region, like Turkey and Iran, attempt to use the Kurds for their own purposes. The Kurds are also weakened because they have no central resistance organization. The article reports that there is some hope that conditions for Kurds may be improving in Turkey, if not in Iraq. John Yemma was a reporter and editor at the Boston Globe *and is now the editor of the* Christian Science Monitor.

The Kurds are called "the orphans of the universe."

Hey have been waging an armed struggle against Saddam Hussein's forces in northern Iraq for the past two weeks [March 1991], resuming a long effort to carve out a nation of their own in the highlands between the Black and Caspian seas. And once again, several Kurdish activists said, treachery and betrayal will probably doom the effort.

Mustafa Barzani: Leader of the Kurdish National Movement

Mustafa Barzani (March 3, 1903–March 1, 1979) was the leader of the Kurdish national movement for half of the twentieth century. The frequent incidence of wholesale sellout of Kurds by regional as well as Western powers throughout his lifetime corroborated the credence of his incisive and oft-quoted dictum, "The Kurds have no friends but their mountains." . . .

Barzani spent most of his life fighting various governments partitioning Kurdistan. The life-long odyssey of his struggle began in 1907 when he was barely three years old. At that age, he and his mother were incarcerated at Mosul Prison in the aftermath of a raid on their region by the Ottoman Turkish forces led by Muhamed Fadil Pasha Daghistani. His father was subsequently brought to the same city to face the gallows. Not only did he fight successive Iraqi regimes, be they under Ottoman or British rule or independent, but he also pursued the struggle inside Iranian Kurdistan, where

Aziz Shyrzad, for instance, visited the Iranian border town of Qasr-e-Shirin last week. Iran, he reported, is supporting Shiite [an Islamic denomination, often in conflict with the ruling Sunni denomination] rebels inside Iraq, but the better-organized Kurdish rebels are being kept under Tehran's tight control.

Washed Up

To Shyrzad and other Kurds, it was another example of the Kurdish cause being exploited by rival nations and of the Kurds consequently getting no closer to achieving nationhood.

Like dozens of previous uprisings, Shyrzad said, "this one is washed up."

"I'm afraid this is typical of what happens to the Kurdish resistance," said Alexander Dawoody, a Boston Kurdish activist

he participated in the founding of the ephemeral Kurdish Republic of Mahabad by Qazi Muhammed in 1946. In the wake of the collapse of the nascent republic, Barzani and his men set out on daring march into the Soviet Union on foot for a sojourn of a dozen years before they returned to Iraqi Kurdistan in 1959. A bloody coup in Baghdad brought the Ba'thist regime to power in 1963, and Barzani had to fight back collaborating combatant units of Iraqi and Syrian armies in Iraqi Kurdistan. The concluding episode of this odyssey was the collapse of the hitherto most formidable and momentous Kurdish liberation movement when, in 1975, reconciled Iran and Iraq joined force in fighting it after the shah of Iran and then Iraqi vice president Saddam Hussein personally signed the Accord of Algiers. Mustafa Barzani had to bid another farewell, which unbeknownst to him would be his last, to his cherished land and made for the United States this time. He died in Washington several years later after a bout with cancer on March 1, 1979.

Ahmed Ferhadi, "Introduction," Mustafa Barzani and the Kurdish Liberation Movement, *by Massoud Barzani. New York: Palgrave Macmillan, 2003, p. 1.*

who was in contact with Shyrzad by telephone yesterday. "No one wants to allow us real independence."

After two weeks of bloody sieges in Basra, Karbala and other southern cities, Baghdad appears to have gained the upper hand in the region against Shiite Muslims.

The situation is less clear in northern Iraq, however, where Kurds have long challenged the Baghdad government. There were reports of continued Kurdish rebel activity around Mosul, Kirkuk and Sulimaniyya yesterday.

For the Kurds, the fight against Saddam Hussein is the latest chapter in a struggle they have waged for hundreds of years.

The closest they ever got to independence was in 1920 when the Treaty of Sevres promised a Kurdish state based in the eastern portion of what later became the nation of Turkey. But three years later—after Turkish nationalist Kemal Ataturk came to power and asserted control over the Anatolian Peninsula—the Treaty of Lausanne superseded Sevres and made no mention of Kurdistan.

Since then, Kurds have staged rebellions aimed at achieving nationhood in the 85,000- to 150,000-square-mile region where they predominate. This has set them variously against the governments of Turkey, Iran and Iraq, all of which have used military means to crush Kurdish insurgents over the years.

Each of these nations has also used the Kurdish cause to put pressure on a nearby rival. The Iraqi government, for instance, supported Iranian Kurds until 1975. The Iranians supported Iraqi Kurds throughout the 1980–88 war with Iraq—and are doing so again. Syria houses Kurdish rebels that have fought the Turkish government.

"But they never really intend to see an independent Kurdistan," Dawoody said.

Shared Oppression

The majority of the 26 million Kurds are Sunni Muslims, five to 10 percent are Shiites, less than 1 percent are Christian and the rest are adherents of pre-Islamic sects, according to Mehrdad Izady, a Harvard lecturer and specialist in Kurdish demography.

"It is a shared heritage," Izady said. "In many ways, oppression is the unifying factor. If you remove the oppression, Kurdish culture might not be as strong a glue as it is now."

History's most illustrious Kurd was Saladin, who in the 12th century led an Islamic army that recaptured Jerusalem. In modern times, Mustapha Barzani carried on a 20-year armed struggle against Iran and Iraq. The Kurdish leader died in exile in Washington in 1979.

Barzani once referred to his people as the "orphans of the universe"—a description Kurds now frequently use to describe their plight.

One problem for Kurdish nationalists is that their efforts are as divided as their homeland. There is no recognized umbrella

Kurdish refugees reach the top of a mountain near their destination of Turkey, after fleeing Saddam Hussein's forces in northern Iraq in 1991. © Patrick Robert/Sygma/Corbis.

group for the Kurds along the lines of the Palestine Liberation Organization for Palestinians.

Instead, most rebel groups are set up along tribal lines. The Kurdish Democratic Party, for instance, is made up mostly of members of the Barzani tribe. The Patriotic Union of Kurdistan is mostly of the Jalal Talabani tribe. The Kurdish Workers Party is the only major group that is not tribally based, but its Marxist ideology and its violent activities against the Turkish government limit its appeal among mainstream Kurds.

More than half the Kurdish population live in eastern Turkey. The ancient city of Diyarbakir is the chief urban center of Turkish Kurdistan.

Just after Iraq invaded Kuwait [in August 1990], Turkey massed troops on the Iraqi border and said it would intervene in Iraq if attacked. That never happened. There have been new reports, however, of Turkish interest in seeing a Kurdish state set up in northern Iraq.

Past Turkish governments outlawed the Kurdish language and demanded that the Kurds be referred to as "mountain Turks."

But in recent months, the government of President Turgut Ozal has eased up somewhat, allowing the language to be used and holding talks with Kurdish opposition groups.

Change in Turkish Policy

"We are pretty optimistic about this," said Bahktiar Zhudi, director of Kurdish Relief Aid, a humanitarian organization based in Palo Alto, Calif. "Turkey is a key player, and if it doesn't have a hidden agenda, we are in a better position than we have been in for many years."

Izady said he thinks the change in Turkish policy could be a recognition that Kurdish population growth is so outstripping Turkish growth that in 35 years the Kurds may constitute a majority of Turkey's population. In his view, Ozal is beginning to make accommodations for this fact.

Vera Saeedpour, curator of the Kurdish Library in Brooklyn, N.Y., had a more cynical view. She saw it as a Turkish attempt to co-opt Kurdish groups in an effort to carve out a Kurdish region, under Turkish control, from northern Iraq.

"It's one of those ideas that would serve the Turks but not the Kurds," she said.

Still, Turkey's policies toward the Kurds have been moderate compared with what has occurred in Iraq, where 20 percent of the population is Kurdish. In the 1970s, Iraqi jets bombed Kurdish villages. There was a lull during the Iran-Iraq war, but just after a cease-fire was signed between Tehran and Baghdad in 1988 Saddam Hussein mounted a military campaign against the Iraqi Kurds.

Poison gas was used on Halabja and other Kurdish villages, according to documentation provided by the Physicians for Human Rights. Estimates of those killed in the attacks run into the thousands, with half a million displaced from their homes. Saddam Hussein's recently appointed interior minister, Ali Hassan Majid, led that campaign against the Kurds.

Kurdish Graves Are Exhumed in Iraq

Middle East Watch and Physicians for Human Rights

In the following viewpoint, two human rights organizations—Middle East Watch and Physicians for Human Rights—jointly report on the exhumation of graves in Iraq in 1991. These graves were believed to contain the bodies of Kurdish victims of Iraq's genocidal campaign against the Kurds, also called the Anfal campaign. The viewpoint describes the state of each of four disinterred skeletons.

Date of Disinterment: December 27–28, 1991
    Location: Saywan Cemetery, Martyr's Hill
Sulaymaniyah, Iraq
Date of Examination: December 28, 1991
Location: Sulaymaniyah City Morgue
Persons Responsible for Excavation and Examination:
Karen Burns
Burney McClurkan
Clyde C. Snow

Middle East Watch and Physicians for Human Rights, "Human Skeletal Remains Exhumed from Saywan Cemetery, Sulaymaniyah, Iraq, on December 27–28, 1991," *Unquiet Graves: The Search for the Disappeared in Iraqi Kurdistan*, February 1992, pp. 37–41. Copyright © 1992 by Middle East Watch and Physicians for Human Rights. All rights reserved. Reproduced by permission.

Pamela Blotner

Eric Stover

Background: The entire day of 27 December was spent at Saywan Cemetery in an area known as the "Hill of Martyrs." Many unidentified persons were buried in this part of the cemetery. Some of the unidentified were execution victims whose bodies had been given to the cemetery workers to bury in secret. A grave digger who was present to locate some of these graves explained that he did the best he could to bury the victims properly with the restrictions given. Without the help of the family, the clothing was not removed and bodies were not washed or shrouded according to custom. The victims were, however, placed in the proper position in the ground and the graves were marked by rough slabs of stone at the head and foot. Many of the headstones were dabbed with blue paint to indicate that the remains were unidentified.

On December 27, two graves (No. 1 and No. 2) were opened side-by-side. The shallowest burial—designated No. 2—was removed. On the same day, a third grave—designated No. 3—was opened across the road from the first two and the remains were removed.

On December 28, the remains were removed from grave No. 1. This grave was approximately a meter deeper than grave No. 2. Grave No. 4 was opened also and a fourth set of remains was disinterred.

All four skeletons were cleaned at the Sulaymaniyah City Morgue on December 28. They are described by number in the following section.

Grave No. 1, Saywan Cemetery

Summary: This grave was deeper and older than the adjacent grave, No. 2. It appears to be a traditional burial in that no clothes or sewing threads are evident. It also appears to have been buried much longer than the others in that the bones are markedly deteriorated. It was determined that this was not one of the execution victims and examination was curtailed.

Skeletal Description: The outer cortex of bone is separated and breaking away. The smaller bones are incomplete and friable.

Dental Description: None

Race: Caucasian

Sex: Male

Age at Death: Elderly

Stature: Not established

Trauma: None noted

Grave No. 2, Saywan Cemetery

Summary: The skeleton is that of a young man with a bullet entry wound in the dorsal aspect of the skull. The exit wound is through the upper neck. There is some crowding of the anterior teeth and evidence of a broken nose. Clothes are present.

Skeletal Description: The bone is free of all soft tissue, deeply stained, and without cortical erosion.

Handedness: There is evidence that he was right-handed.

Dental Description: Third molars are erupted. Caries present on mandibular second molars (#18 & #31). Anterior malalignment: maxillary lateral incisors both overlap the lateral margins of central incisors. There is lingual displacement of one mandibular central incisor.

Race: Caucasian

Sex: Male

Age at Death: Young adult, 17–22 years old. The vault sutures are patent, S1/2 is unfused, the medial clavicle is unfused, and other late-closing epiphyses are in the final stages of fusion.

Stature: 5'8" or 173 cm. (range 167.53–179.53 cm.)

Pre-mortem Disease/Trauma: The nasal bridge is prominent and deviated to the left, suggesting an old, healed nasal fracture. Otherwise, the skeleton displays no osseous pathologies that would be reflected in the deceased's medical history.

Post-mortem Trauma: An ovoid entry wound is located 40 mm. posterior to the coronal suture and 35 mm. lateral to the sagittal suture in the right parietal bone. The wound measures

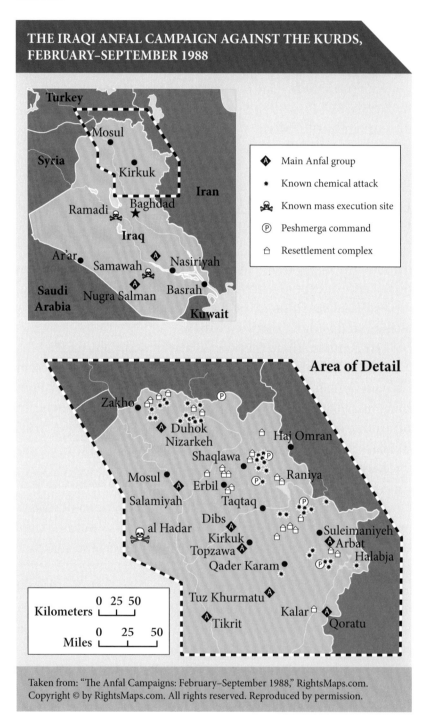

THE IRAQI ANFAL CAMPAIGN AGAINST THE KURDS,
FEBRUARY–SEPTEMBER 1988

Turkey

Mosul

Syria

Kirkuk

Iran

Ramadi Baghdad

Iraq

Ar'ar Samawah Nasiriyah

Saudi Nugra Salman Basrah
Arabia

Kuwait

⬢ Main Anfal group

✱ Known chemical attack

☠ Known mass execution site

Ⓟ Peshmerga command

⌂ Resettlement complex

Area of Detail

Zakho

Duhok
Nizarkeh Haj Omran

Shaqlawa

Mosul Raniya
Erbil

Salamiyah Taqtaq

Dibs
al Hadar Suleimaniyeh
Kirkuk Arbat
Topzawa Halabja

Qader Karam

Tuz Khurmatu

Kilometers 0 25 50

Kalar Qoratu
Tikrit

Miles 0 25 50

Taken from: "The Anfal Campaigns: February–September 1988," RightsMaps.com.
Copyright © by RightsMaps.com. All rights reserved. Reproduced by permission.

11 mm. transversely and 9 mm. from anterior to posterior. An exit wound is located in the base of the skull. It is an irregular defect measuring approximately 16 mm. by 11 mm. and located lateral to the left mandibular fossa. There is traumatic damage associated with the gunshot wound involving the lateral superior articular facet of C2 and the anterior wall of the transverse foramen of C3.

Grave No. 3, Saywan Cemetery

Summary: The skeleton is that of an adult woman who has borne children. There are no visible wounds on the skeleton. The clothes from this woman were identified by the assistant to the pathologist, Anwar Ali Mohammad. Mohammad's description of the woman was consistent with the skeletal description to the extent possible. The woman's morgue records were located by Mohammad and the name of the deceased was said to be Gula Karim Ahmed. She had been brought to the morgue by Iraqi soldiers on November 24, 1989, after being hung to death by a rope. From the morgue, her body had been sent to the cemetery for anonymous burial.

Skeletal Description: The bone is exposed but still in association with both skin and muscle tissue. The conditions of the burial are consistent with anaerobic decomposition. (Thick, nonorganic clay soil, soaked by a slow water flow from an uphill fountain.) The sternum is fused; L5 is fused with the sacrum, early stage osteophytosis is apparent on the vertebral bodies, parturition scarring is present as well as deep preauricular sulcus.

Handedness: The person was right handed.

Dental Description: Adult dentition with attrition extending into the dentin and extensive periodontal disease.

Race: Caucasian

Sex: Female

Age at Death: Adult, 31–39 years old.

Stature: 5'2" or 157 cm. (range 150–164 cm.).

Hair: Dark brown, in braids.
Trauma: None apparent.

Grave No. 4, Saywan Cemetery

Summary: This skeleton is that of an adult man. There is a gunshot wound through the skull. The entrance is in the left side of the skull, exiting on the right. This appears to be a double entry wound, probably from an automatic weapon. One severely eroded projectile was recovered from the interior of the skull. Clothes are present.

Skeletal Description: The bone is free of all soft tissue, deeply stained, and without cortical erosion. The vertebral column is normal; S1/2 is closed; ribs are normal; the body of the sternum is skewed; all postcranial epiphyses are closed and no osteophytosis is apparent.

Handedness: The person was right handed.

Dental Description: Pre-mortem loss of #32 and #16, massive caries of #17.

Race: Caucasian

Sex: Male

Age at Death: Adult, 27–38 years.

Stature: 5'5" or 165 cm. (160–172 cm.).

Trauma: There is an entry wound in the squamous portion of the left temporal bone immediately superior to the left zygomatic process. The wound measures 15 mm. vertically and 16 mm. transversely. The exit wound straddles the posterior segment of the squamous suture and measures 45 mm. transversely and 20 mm. vertically.

Kurds and Shia Muslims Vote Together in Post-Saddam Iraq

Economist

In the following viewpoint, a British news and business magazine reports on elections in Iraq following the ouster of Saddam Hussein by a 2003 American invasion. The Economist *says that Shia Muslims (the majority Muslim denomination in Iraq) and Kurds turned out in large numbers for the election. Sunni Muslims, who had been more supportive of Hussein's rule, were less represented. The magazine reports that rebels failed to disrupt the election, but notes that the insurgency is growing in force, and expresses concern that Iraq might experience even worse sectarian violence, and perhaps even civil war, in the future.*

The insurgents had declared "holy war" on the elections, on any "infidel" who took part in them—and indeed on the very concept of democracy. But on Sunday January 30th [2005], millions of Iraqis defied the bombs and bullets, the threats and the curses, and queued to cast their votes in the country's first elections since the American-led invasion to topple Saddam Hussein in 2003—indeed, the country's first genuine multi-party elections for half a century. Because of the fear of assassination, by and large only the most senior party leaders had done any visible campaigning. The names of most of the 7,000 candidates for the 275-seat Iraqi national assembly, and the location of many polling stations, had been kept secret until the last moment.

Kurds Turn Out in High Numbers

As had been expected, turnout was highest in the Kurdish region in northern Iraq and in the strongholds of Iraq's majority Shia Muslim population. Voters formed long queues to cast their ballots, in some cases chanting and clapping with joy at being granted their first ever chance to choose their government. Some proudly showed their fingers, stained with indelible blue ink (to prevent multiple voting), as they left the polling stations.

Turnout was derisory or zero in many Sunni Muslim[1] areas. But not all: astonishingly, a modest stream of voters was seen in the bombed-out remains of Fallujah, in the deadly "Sunni triangle" west of the capital, which American-led forces recaptured from insurgents in a bloody battle last November [2004]. President George Bush declared the elections a success, while the United Nations' secretary-general, Kofi Annan, congratulated those Iraqis who had plucked up the courage to vote, saying that: "They are voting for the future of their country. They are voting for the day when they will have their destiny in their own hands."

One of the most bloodthirsty insurgent groups, led by Abu Musab al-Zarqawi, a Jordanian affiliated to al-Qaeda [the terrorist group that destroyed the World Trade Center], bragged on the internet that it had been behind a number of suicide-bombings of polling stations, mainly in Baghdad. In all, around 35 people were killed in attacks while the polls were open. Ten British servicemen were missing, believed killed, after a Royal Air Force transport plane crashed near Baghdad on Sunday, possibly due to an attack by insurgents. However, even before voting closed, it had become clear that—as in Afghanistan's presidential election in December—the insurgents had failed to terrorise Iraq's voters into staying at home.

More than 50 Percent Vote

There had been fears in recent days that the rebels were conserving their resources to launch spectacular attacks on polling day. But this seems to have been prevented by stringent security restrictions and the strong presence of troops from the American-led coalition, alongside Iraqi forces. America had boosted its troop levels in Iraq from 138,000 to 150,000 to provide additional security for the elections, in which a total of around 300,000 Iraqi and foreign troops were on guard.

At first, officials from Iraq's electoral commission claimed that as many as 72% of the 13m [million] registered voters had cast ballots. But they later backtracked, saying that perhaps around 8m, or 60% of registered voters, had turned up, and that this was only a preliminary guess. The interim Iraqi government, led by [Ayyad] Allawi, had set itself a target of at least a 50% turnout. In addition to the overall turnout figure, close attention will be paid to the participation in Sunni areas: clearly, the Sunnis will be under-represented in the national assembly, but the question is by how much.

The counting of ballots has already begun, though even preliminary results are not expected for about another week. The most likely outcome is that the United Iraqi Alliance (better known by Iraqis as "the Shia house," "the clerics' list" or simply "169," after its number on the vast ballot paper) will do best, since it has the tacit blessing of Grand Ayatollah Ali al-Sistani, the most influential cleric among the 60% of Iraqis who are Shia Muslims. A catch-all Kurdish Alliance is sure to sweep up the vast majority of Kurdish votes. And a list headed by Mr Allawi, a secular Shia, may do better than was once expected, thanks to his image as a tough, steady leader.

The Insurgency Continues

Mr Allawi's group is more secular and less sectarian than the Shia house, though the latter's leaders insist they are not seeking an Iranian-style theocracy: "We will have no turbans in the

A woman displays her finger marked with indelible ink after voting in the Iraqi elections of 2005. © AP Images.

government," says one. The likely outcome of the election is a coalition involving the Shia house, the Kurds, Mr Allawi's lot and several Sunni Arab-led parties. In recent days there has been speculation that Mr Allawi may succeed in persuading the other parties to let him stay on as prime minister, though there may be a long period of wrangling before the new government emerges.

Seats in the new assembly will be allocated by pure proportional representation. It must first vote for a president and two vice-presidents who, in turn, as a presidential council, must unanimously choose the prime minister. He must then choose a government, which must be endorsed by a simple majority of the assembly's members. Perhaps more important, the assembly must oversee the writing of a new and final constitution, to be drafted by mid-August and endorsed in a referendum by mid-October, leading to a full general election under new rules by mid-December (though the rules allow for some slippage). If two-thirds of voters in three provinces reject the new constitution, the process must start again. That gives both the Kurds and the Sunni Arabs a veto.

All this, however, seems immaterial while the insurgency rages, at a rate much higher than a year ago. American officers say their troops are subjected to some 70 attacks a day. Since the invasion, around 1,100 have died in combat and another 250 or so in accidents. Even more grimly, the tally of Iraqi civilian deaths continues to rise inexorably. IraqBodyCount, an anti-war but fastidious group, reckons that 15,000–18,000 Iraqi civilians have been killed since March 2003.

By a Brookings Institution estimate based mainly on Pentagon briefings, some 32,000 insurgents have been killed or captured since the conventional phase of the war ended in April 2003. Yet the number of active insurgents, though hard to count, has plainly continued to swell. The head of Iraq's intelligence service suggested earlier this month that there were 40,000 hard-core rebels, with another 160,000-odd Iraqis helping them out. That is several times the standard, albeit rough, estimate of a year ago.

So the new government will face colossal challenges: the huge numbers of frustrated, unemployed Iraqi youths are a willing pool of recruits, not just for insurgent groups but also for the armed gangs and criminal underworld that hold sway in many parts of the country. A rebellious young cleric, Muqtada al-Sadr, and his thuggish militia, known as the Mahdi Army, have been lying low since Mr Sistani talked them out of their rebellion against American occupation late last summer. But they control swathes of the centre and south, and could rise up again if he or his group were cut out of a power-sharing deal.

And while the Kurdish north is the safest part of Iraq, tension is growing over the bitterly contested and oil-rich city of Kirkuk, to where many of the Kurds displaced in Saddam's brutal Arabisation campaign are returning.

The American Timeline

The insurgents will do their utmost to provoke sectarian warfare between Kurds and Sunnis, and Sunnis and Shias, or among any of the country's other ethnic and religious groups. Any one of several potential flashpoints might trigger wider unrest that, unless the new government handles things skillfully, could push Iraq towards civil war and even a break-up.

Mr Allawi argues that, provided the Americans do not cut and run, the insurgency can be contained, if not beaten. The main plan is to beef up the home-grown Iraqi forces (now totalling 127,000 against an eventual goal of 273,000), enabling the Americans and their allies to wind down their troop numbers. This, within the next few years, is a false hope. The Iraqi forces are utterly feeble. At present, only some 5,000 of them are a match for the insurgents.

Besides giving more moderate Sunnis fair representation on the new presidential council and on the committee drafting the new constitution, the new government must also reach out to spokesmen for the insurgency, which is far from monolithic. Most insurgents are above all nationalists. The government might accommodate many of them if they could be convinced that the Americans were certain to leave—if not immediately, at least soon. A new government could ask foreign troops to leave; but that is barely conceivable in the short run, because any government is bound, for now, to rely heavily on American force for its mere physical survival.

A rough timetable could be spelled out: some voices in the Sunni rejectionist camp have aired the possibility of a ceasefire if the Americans promised, in principle, to leave in, say, six months. That is unthinkable for the moment but may offer a chink of light for negotiations. Mr Bush told Friday's *New York Times* that he would withdraw American troops if asked but that the political leaders likely to win the election understood the need to keep them for now.

Note

1. Sunni is a Muslim denomination. Saddam Hussein was a Sunni, and Sunnis were among the strongest opponents of the new American-backed Iraqi government.

CHAPTER 2

Controversies Surrounding the Kurds

Chapter Exercises

IRAQI OPINION IN 2004 OF THE 2003 US-LED INVASION			
	Kurds	Arabs	All
US-Led Invasion			
Was right	87%	40%	48%
Was wrong	9%	46%	39%
Liberated Iraq	82%	33%	42%
Humiliated Iraq	11%	48%	41%
Presence of US-Led Coalition Forces			
Support	82%	30%	39%
Oppose	12%	60%	51%
Attacks on US-Led Coalition Forces			
Acceptable	2%	21%	17%
Unacceptable	96%	74%	78%

Taken from: Gary Langer, "Poll: Iraqis Report Better Postwar Life," ABCNews.com. March 15, 2004.

1. Analyze the Table

Question 1: Which group is most supportive of the US-led invasion of Iraq? Based on your reading, why is this the case?

Question 2: The total percentage of Iraqis who support the presence of coalition forces is 39 percent, far closer to the 30 percent of Arabs who support coalition forces than to the 82 percents of Kurds who do so. Why do Arabs have more influence on the overall figure? In your answer, consider the population makeup of Iraq.

Question 3: Do you believe the United States should have invaded Iraq in 2003? Do the opinions expressed by Arabs and Kurds affect your stance? Explain your answers.

2. Writing Prompt

Imagine you are a political blogger. Write a post in which you argue that Saddam Hussein's actions in the Anfal campaign against the Kurds did or did not constitute genocide. Use evidence from the viewpoints in this chapter to support your position.

3. Group Activity

Form two groups for a debate. One side should attempt to support and one side should attempt to refute the statement: "The United States has acted in the best interests of the Kurdish people."

Saddam Hussein's Actions Against the Kurds Constitute Genocide

Human Rights Watch

In the following viewpoint, Human Rights Watch (HRW), an international human rights organization, argues that the 1987–1988 Iraqi Anfal campaign against the Kurds constituted a genocide. HRW says that Anfal was in part a counterinsurgency campaign against Kurds, but that it also functioned as a genocidal effort to eliminate ethnic Kurds. HRW points out that the Iraqis used chemical weapons and other murderous violence against civilians. They say civilians were sent into camps, where they were processed and often murdered based not on their actions, but simply on their ethnicity. HRW also presents evidence that the director of the Anfal campaign, Ali Hassan al-Majid, was motivated by racial animus against the Kurds.

This report is a narrative account of a campaign of extermination against the Kurds of northern Iraq. It is the product of over a year and a half of research, during which a team of Middle East Watch researchers has analyzed several tons of captured Iraqi government documents and carried out field interviews with more than 350 witnesses, most of them survivors of the 1988 campaign known as Anfal. It concludes that in that year the Iraqi regime committed the crime of genocide.

Gross Violations of Human Rights

Anfal—"the Spoils"—is the name of the eighth *sura* [chapter] of the Koran. It is also the name given by the Iraqis to a series of military actions which lasted from February 23 until September 6, 1988. While it is impossible to understand the Anfal campaign without reference to the final phase of the 1980–1988 Iran-Iraq War, Anfal was not merely a function of that war. Rather, the winding-up of the conflict on Iraq's terms was the immediate historical circumstance that gave Baghdad the opportunity to bring to a climax its longstanding efforts to bring the Kurds to heel. For the Iraqi regime's anti-Kurdish drive dated back some fifteen years or more, well before the outbreak of hostilities between Iran and Iraq.

Anfal was also the most vivid expression of the "special powers" granted to Ali Hassan al-Majid, a cousin of President Saddam Hussein and secretary general of the Northern Bureau of Iraq's Ba'ath Arab Socialist Party. From March 29, 1987 until April 23, 1989, al-Majid was granted power that was equivalent, in Northern Iraq, to that of the President himself, with authority over all agencies of the state. Al-Majid, who is known to this day to Kurds as "Ali Anfal" or "Ali Chemical," was the overlord of the Kurdish genocide. Under his command, the central actors in Anfal were the First and Fifth Corps of the regular Iraqi Army, the General Security Directorate (*Mudiriyat al-Amn al-Ameh*) and Military Intelligence (*Istikhbarat*). The pro-government Kurdish militia known as the National Defense Battalions, or *jahsh,* assisted in important auxiliary tasks. But the integrated resources of the entire military, security and civilian apparatus of the Iraqi state were deployed, in al-Majid's words, "to solve the Kurdish problem and slaughter the saboteurs."

The campaigns of 1987–1989 were characterized by the following gross violations of human rights:

- mass summary executions and mass disappearance of many tens of thousands of non-combatants, including large numbers of women and children, and sometimes the entire population of villages;
- the widespread use of chemical weapons, including mustard gas and the nerve agent GB, or Sarin, against the town of Halabja as well as dozens of Kurdish villages, killing many thousands of people, mainly women and children;
- the wholesale destruction of some 2,000 villages, which are described in government documents as having been "burned," "destroyed," "demolished" and "purified," as well as at least a dozen larger towns and administrative centers (*nahyas* and *qadhas*);
- the wholesale destruction of civilian objects by Army engineers, including all schools, mosques, wells and other non-residential structures in the targeted villages, and a number of electricity substations;
- looting of civilian property and farm animals on a vast scale by army troops and pro-government militia;
- arbitrary arrest of all villagers captured in designated "prohibited areas" (*manateq al-mahdoureh*), despite the fact that these were their own homes and lands;
- arbitrary jailing and warehousing for months, in conditions of extreme deprivation, of tens of thousands of women, children and elderly people, without judicial order or any cause other than their presumed sympathies for the Kurdish opposition. Many hundreds of them were allowed to die of malnutrition and disease;
- forced displacement of hundreds of thousands of villagers upon the demolition of their homes, their release from jail or return from exile; these civilians were trucked into areas of Kurdistan far from their homes and dumped there by the army with only minimal govern-

mental compensation or none at all for their destroyed property, or any provision for relief, housing, clothing or food, and forbidden to return to their villages of origin on pain of death. In these conditions, many died within a year of their forced displacement;

- destruction of the rural Kurdish economy and infrastructure.

Like Nazi Germany, the Iraqi regime concealed its actions in euphemisms. Where Nazi officials spoke of "executive measures," "special actions" and "resettlement in the east," Ba'athist bureaucrats spoke of "collective measures," "return to the national ranks" and "resettlement in the south." But beneath the euphemisms, Iraq's crimes against the Kurds amount to genocide, the "intent to destroy, in whole or in part, a national, ethnical, racial or religious group, as such." [as defined in the United Nations convention on the Prevention and Punishment of the Crime of Genocide] . . .

The Attack on the Kurds

The Anfal campaign began . . . with a massive military assault on the PUK [Patriotic Union of Kurdistan] headquarters at Sergalou-Bergalou on the night of February 23, 1988. Anfal would have eight stages in all, seven of them directed at areas under the control of the PUK. The KDP [Kurdish Democratic Party]-controlled areas in the northwest of Iraqi Kurdistan, which the regime regarded as a lesser threat, were the target of the Final Anfal operation in late August and early September, 1988.

The Iraqi authorities did nothing to hide the campaign from public view. On the contrary, as each phase of the operation triumphed, its successes were trumpeted with the same propaganda fanfare that attended the victorious battles in the Iran-Iraq War. Even today [1993], Anfal is celebrated in the official Iraqi media. The fifth anniversary in 1993 of the fall of Sergalou and Bergalou on March 19, 1988 was the subject of banner headlines. . . .

Ali Hassan al-Majid: War Criminal and Cousin of Saddam Hussein

Known as "Chemical Ali," Ali Hassan al-Majid was the cousin of Iraqi leader, President Saddam Hussein, and a powerful member of the Iraqi government. A general in the Iraqi army, he acquired his nickname because of the use of chemical weapons and other atrocities he ordered against the Kurds in the late 1980s. During the 2003 American-led invasion of Iraq, he was the leader of the Iraqi army in the south.

Majid began his career in the Iraqi army as a driver and motorcycle messenger. After his cousin Hussein took power, Majid held a number of positions in his government. . . .

Majid's first known war crime occurred in 1983. He killed people who lived in the village of Dujail, the home village of the assassins who made an attempt on the life of Hussein. Because of such actions, Majid was a trusted advisor of Hussein.

In 1987, Majid was named a head for Hussein in northern Iraq. He was the secretary general of the Northern Bureau of the Ba'ath Party, the ruling party in Iraq. In this position, he controlled parts of the Iraqi Army, military intelligence, and security.

As the military leader in northern Iraq, Majid committed what many human rights observers and others consider a significant violation. During the failed Kurdish rebellions in northern Iraq in 1988

Each stage of Anfal followed roughly the same pattern. It characteristically began with chemical attacks from the air on both civilian and *peshmerga* [armed Kurdish fighters] targets, accompanied by a military blitz against PUK or KDP military bases and fortified positions. The deadly cocktail of mustard and nerve gases was much more lethal against civilians than against the *peshmerga,* some of whom had acquired gas masks and other rudimentary defenses. In the village of Sayw Senan (Second

and 1991, Majid used chemical weapons, torture, and committed other atrocities against the Kurds. . . .

The Kurds were not the only population that was targeted for destruction by Majid. During the 1990 invasion of Kuwait by Iraq, he was named the military governor of Kuwait and destroyed Kuwaiti villages, looted, raped, and pillaged the people.

After the war ended in 1991 with Iraq's loss, Majid was named interior minister and appointed to the ruling Revolutionary Council. He was sent to the south of Iraq to suppress the revolt of Iraqi Shi'ite Muslims. Under his orders, they were run over by tanks and executed en masse by the Iraqi army. During the 1990s, he was also involved in the destruction of the Marsh Arab population, reducing them from 250,000 to 40,000 by gassing, bombing, torture, and forced exile. . . .

During the 2003 invasion of Iraq by the United States and its allies, Majid was in charge of Iraqi troops in the southern part of the country. Some believed that this was perhaps meant to intimidate the invading allies because of his reputation for using chemical weapons. While it did lead resistance to U.S. troops in the south, by early April 2003, there was not any use of chemical weapons. . . .

In early April of 2003, CNN reported that the British military had found the body of Majid. He was said to have died in a coalition airstrike on the city of Basra. The reports were unconfirmed by the U.S. military, although they conceded that it was "likely" Majid had died in the attack.

A. Petruso, "Ali Hassan al-Majid," Gale Student Resources in Context. Detroit: Gale, 2003.

Anfal), more than eighty civilians died; in Goktapa (Fourth Anfal), the death toll was more than 150; in Wara (Fifth Anfal) it was thirty-seven. In the largest chemical attack of all, the March 16 bombing of the Kurdish town of Halabja, between 3,200 and 5,000 residents died. As a city, Halabja was not technically part of Anfal—the raid was carried out in reprisal for its capture by *peshmerga* supported by Iranian Revolutionary Guards—but it was very much part of the Kurdish genocide.

After the initial assault, ground troops and *jahsh* [pro-government Kurdish militia] enveloped the target area from all sides, destroying all human habitation in their path, looting household possessions and farm animals and setting fire to homes, before calling in demolition crews to finish the job. . . . Convoys of army trucks stood by to transport the villagers to nearby holding centers and transit camps, while the *jahsh* combed the hillsides to track down anyone who had escaped. (Some members of the militia, an asset of dubious reliability to the regime, also saved thousands of lives by spiriting people away to safety or helping them across army lines.) Secret police combed the towns, cities and complexes to hunt down Anfal fugitives, and in several cases lured them out of hiding with false offers of amnesty and a "return to the national ranks"—a promise that now concealed a more sinister meaning.

More than Counterinsurgency

To this point, Anfal had many of the characteristics of a counterinsurgency campaign, albeit an unusually savage one. And captured Iraqi documents suggest that during the initial combat phase, counterinsurgency goals were uppermost in the minds of the troops and their commanding officers. To be sure, Iraq—like any other sovereign nation—had legitimate interests in combating insurgency. But the fact that Anfal was, by the narrowest definition, a counterinsurgency, does nothing to diminish the fact that it was also an act of genocide. There is nothing mutually exclusive about counterinsurgency and genocide. Indeed, one may be the instrument used to consummate the other. Article I of the Genocide Convention affirms that "genocide, whether committed in time of peace or in time of war, is a crime under international law." Summarily executing noncombatant or captured members of an ethnical-national group as such is not a legitimate wartime or counterinsurgency measure, regardless of the nature of the conflict.

In addition to this argument of principle, many features of Anfal far transcend the realm of counterinsurgency. These include, first of all, the simple facts of what happened after the military goals of the operation had been accomplished:

- the mass murder and disappearance of many tens of thousands of non-combatants—50,000 by the most conservative estimate, and possibly twice that number;
- the use of chemical weapons against non-combatants in dozens of locations, killing thousands and terrifying many more into abandoning their homes;
- the near-total destruction of family and community assets and infrastructure, including the entire agricultural mainstay of the rural Kurdish economy;
- the literal abandonment, in punishing conditions, of thousands of women, children and elderly people, resulting in the deaths of many hundreds. Those who survived did so largely due to the clandestine help of nearby Kurdish townspeople.

Second, there is the matter of how Anfal was organized as a bureaucratic enterprise. Viewed as a counterinsurgency, each episode of Anfal had a distinct beginning and an end, and its conduct was in the hands of the regular army and the *jahsh* militia. But these agencies were quickly phased out of the picture, and the captured civilians were transferred to an entirely separate bureaucracy for processing and final disposal. Separate institutions were involved—such as *Amn, Istikhbarat*, the Popular Army (a type of home guard) and the Ba'ath Party itself. And the infrastructure of prison camps and death convoys was physically remote from the combat theater, lying well outside the Kurdistan Autonomous Region. Tellingly, the killings were not in any sense concurrent with the counterinsurgency: the detainees were murdered several days or even weeks after the armed forces had secured their goals. Finally, there is the question of intent, which goes to the heart of the notion of genocide. Documentary materials captured from the Iraqi intelligence agencies demonstrate with great clarity that the mass killings, disappearances and forced relocations associated with Anfal and the other anti-Kurdish campaigns of 1987–1989 were planned in coherent fashion. While power over these campaigns was highly centralized, their success depended on the orchestration of the efforts of a large number of agencies and institutions at the local, regional and national level, from the Office of the Presidency of the Republic on down to the lowliest *jahsh* unit.

Ali Hassan al-Majid

The official at the center of this great bureaucratic web, of course, was Ali Hassan al-Majid, and in him the question of intent is apparent on a second, extremely important level. A number of audiotapes were made of meetings between al-Majid and his aides from 1987 to 1989. These tapes were examined by four independent experts, to establish their authenticity and to confirm that the principal speaker was al-Majid. Al-Majid was known to have a distinctive, high-pitched voice and the regional accent of his Tikrit district origins; both these features were recognized without hesitation by those Iraqis consulted by Middle East Watch. As a public figure who frequently appears on radio and television in Iraq, his voice is well known to many Iraqis. One Iraqi consulted on this subject pointed out that the principal speaker on the many hours of recordings in Middle East Watch's possession spoke with authority and used obscene language. In contrast, he said: "Others in those meetings were courteous and respectful with fearful tones, especially when they addressed al-Majid himself." Al-Majid, two experts noted, was often referred to by his familiar nickname, "Abu Hassan."

The tapes contain evidence of a bitter racial animus against the Kurds on the part of the man who, above any other, plotted their destruction. "Why should I let them live there like donkeys who don't know anything?" al-Majid asks in one meeting. "What did we ever get from them?" On another occasion, speaking in the same vein: "I said probably we will find some good ones among [the Kurds] . . . but we didn't, never." And elsewhere,

Human skulls and clothes are found at a mass grave in the al-Samawa desert in the Muthanna province, Iraq, in 2005. Evidence dates them to the Anfal campaign of 1987–1988. © AP Images.

"I will smash their heads. These kind of dogs, we will crush their heads." And again, "Take good care of them? No, I will bury them with bulldozers."

Loyalty to the regime offered no protection from al-Majid's campaigns. Nor did membership in the pro-government *jahsh*. Al-Majid even boasted of threatening militia leaders with chemical weapons if they refused to evacuate their villages. Ethnicity and physical location were all that mattered, and these factors became coterminous when the mass killings took place in 1988.

The 1987 village clearances were wholly directed at government-controlled areas, and thus had nothing whatever to do with counterinsurgency. If the former residents of these areas refused to accept government-assigned housing in a *mujamma'a*, and took refuge instead in a *peshmerga*-controlled area—as many did—they too were liable to be killed during Anfal. The same applied to other smaller minorities. In the October 1987 census, many Assyrian and Chaldean Christians—an Aramaic-speaking people of ancient origin—refused the government's demands that they designate themselves either as Arabs or Kurds. Those who declined to be Arabs were automatically treated as Kurds. And, during the Final Anfal in Dohuk governorate, where most Christians were concentrated, they were in fact dealt with by the regime even more severely than their Kurdish neighbors. Those few Turkomans, a Turkic-speaking minority, who fought with the Kurdish *peshmerga* were not spared, because they too were deemed to have become Kurds.

Almost continuously for the previous two decades, the Ba'ath-led government had engaged in a campaign of Arabization of Kurdish regions. The armed resistance this inspired was Kurdish in character and composition. In 1988, the rebels and all those deemed to be sympathizers were therefore treated as Kurds who had to be wiped out, once and for all. Whether they were combatants or not was immaterial; as far as the government was concerned they were all "bad Kurds," who had not come over to the side of the government. . . .

Firing Squads

Under the terms of al-Majid's June 1987 directives, death was the automatic penalty for any male of an age to bear arms who was found in an Anfal area. At the same time, no one was supposed to go before an Anfal firing squad without first having his or her case individually examined. There is a great deal of documentary evidence to support this view, beginning with a presidential order of October 15, 1987 . . . that "the names of persons who are to be subjected to a general/blanket judgment must not be listed collectively. Rather, refer to them or treat them in your correspondence on an individual basis." The effects of this order are reflected in the lists that the Army and *Amn* compiled of Kurds arrested during Anfal, which note each person's name, sex, age, place of residence and place of capture.

The processing of the detainees took place in a network of camps and prisons. The first temporary holding centers were in operation, under the control of military intelligence, as early as March 15, 1988; by about the end of that month, the mass disappearances had begun in earnest, peaking in mid-April and early May. Most of the detainees went to a place called Topzawa, a Popular Army camp on the outskirts of Kirkuk—the city where Ali Hassan al-Majid had his headquarters. Some went to the Popular Army barracks in Tikrit. Women and children were trucked on from Topzawa to a separate camp in the town of Dibs; between 6,000 and 8,000 elderly detainees were taken to the abandoned prison of Nugra Salman in the southern desert, where hundreds of them died of neglect, starvation and disease. Badinan prisoners from the Final Anfal went through a separate but parallel system, with most being detained in the huge army fort at Dohuk and the women and children being transferred later to a prison camp in Salamiyeh on the Tigris River close to Mosul.

The majority of the women, children and elderly people were released from the camps after the September 6 [1988] amnesty. But none of the Anfal men were released. Middle East Watch's presumption, based on the testimony of a number of survivors from the Third and bloodiest Anfal, is that they went in large groups before firing squads and were interred secretly outside the Kurdish areas. During the Final Anfal in Badinan, in at least two cases groups of men were executed on the spot after capture by military officers carrying out instructions from their commanders. . . .

Nazi Parallels

While the camp system is evocative of one dimension of the Nazi genocide, the range of execution methods described by Kurdish survivors is uncannily reminiscent of another—the activities of the *Einsatzkommandos,* or mobile killing units, in the Nazi-occupied lands of Eastern Europe. Each of the standard operating techniques used by the *Einsatzkommandos* is documented in the Kurdish case. Some groups of prisoners were lined up, shot from the front and dragged into pre-dug mass graves; others were shoved roughly into trenches and machine-gunned where they stood; others were made to lie down in pairs, sardine-style, next to mounds of fresh corpses, before being killed; others were tied together, made to stand on the lip of the pit, and shot in the back so that they would fall forward into it—a method that was presumably more efficient from the point of view of the killers. Bulldozers then pushed earth or sand loosely over the heaps of corpses. Some of the gravesites contained dozens of separate pits, and obviously contained the bodies of thousands of victims. Circumstantial evidence suggests that the executioners were uniformed members of the Ba'ath Party, or perhaps of Iraq's General Security Directorate (*Amn*).

By the most conservative estimates, 50,000 rural Kurds died during Anfal. While males from approximately fourteen to fifty were routinely killed en masse, a number of questions surround the selection criteria that were used to order the murder of younger children and entire families.

Many thousands of women and children perished, but subject to extreme regional variations, with most being residents of two distinct "clusters" that were affected by the Third and Fourth Anfals. . . .

Whatever the precise reasons, it is clear from captured Iraqi documents that the intelligence agencies scrutinized at least some cases individually, and even appealed to the highest authority if they were in doubt about the fate of a particular individual. This suggests that the annihilation process was governed, at least in principle, by rigid bureaucratic norms. But all the evidence suggests that the purpose of these norms was not to rule on a particular person's guilt or innocence of specific charges, but merely to establish whether an individual belonged to the target group that was to be "Anfalized," i.e. Kurds in areas outside government control. At the same time, survivor testimony repeatedly indicates that the rulebook was only adhered to casually in practice. The physical segregation of detainees from Anfal areas by age and sex, as well as the selection of those to be exterminated, was a crude affair, conducted without any meaningful prior process of interrogation or evaluation.

Saddam Hussein's Actions Against the Kurds Were Horrific, but Do Not Constitute Genocide

Patrick E. Tyler

In the following viewpoint, an American journalist reports on traveling to Iraq shortly after the conclusion of the Anfal campaign against the Kurds. He says that Kurds in Iraq have been displaced and that their way of life has been drastically altered, but that they have not suffered a genocide. He suggests that the Anfal campaign was a military attack upon Kurdish insurgents, rather than a genocidal campaign against Kurdish civilians. Patrick Tyler is a former correspondent for the Washington Post *and* New York Times *and author of* A World of Trouble: The White House and the Middle East from the Cold War to the War on Terror.

Genocide, the extermination of a race of people and their culture, the term used by the U.S. Senate to sound the alarm about the fate of the Kurdish people, is not an accurate term for what is happening in this part of Iraq.

Relocation, Not Genocide

But something horrible and historic is indeed being wrought to remake an age-old landscape and the way of life for the 3 million

Kurds in the mountainous north of this war-torn country. They are among some 20 million Kurds scattered through five countries, principally in the contiguous mountain regions of Turkey, Iran and Iraq known as Kurdistan.

The vast majority of Iraq's Kurds are safe in their homes, perhaps safer than when Kurdish guerrillas routinely cut the roads to extract tolls from Kurdish townsfolk, to terrorize local government officials and to kidnap those for whom ransoms might be paid.

Yet life is changing here drastically for the Kurds under a massive and forced relocation program that was accelerated two years ago to break the centuries-old cycle of trouble between rebellious mountain Kurds and town-dwelling Kurds who cooperate with the government. Baghdad is bent not only on depopulating the region but on closing its borders in the high mountains, cutting off Iraqi Kurds from brothers, sisters, cousins in Turkey and Iran.

The relocation program has been compounded by a wave of repression against Kurdish rebels who allied themselves with the hated enemy in the bitter Iran-Iraq war in hopes of winning greater autonomy from Baghdad.

On Sept. 17 [1988], two dozen foreign journalists in five big Soviet MI8 helicopters landed in this decade-old Kurdish resettlement project a few miles from the Turkish border. It was probably an accident of history that forced the authoritarian regime of President Saddam Hussein to allow the world to see what is going on here. The Iraqi government had sent us to the north to prove to the world that chemical weapons were not used in crushing the Kurdish rebel forces.

We, in turn, came here to glean anything we could about what has occurred. After two days of flying hundreds of miles from Kirkuk to Arbil, Dokan, Balisan, Shalaqwa and then to Mosul and from there to Dohuk, Amadiyeh, Zewa, Kani Masi, Batufa and Zakho, it is clear that the major towns and cities of Kurdistan are still standing, unscathed and populated by Kurds who cling to their rich culture under the protection of a government that recognizes some amount of Kurdish autonomy and condones and encourages the preservation of the Kurdish way of life.

Life Goes On

At Batufa, life is going on. But it is not as pretty as the life the Kurds used to live with their flocks in the high valleys—a sort of noble Hobbit land of mud-roof houses covered with spring grass, where men in blousy pants and women in colorful costumes spoke to each other in a unique and lyrical tongue.

It is now illegal in Iraq to have a single house in the mountains and to live within six miles of the border. More than 200 small villages have been demolished in one province, their residents collectivized in "complexes" such as Batufa, built by the Iraqi government to give the Kurds a house, electricity, water and some land to till. An Iraqi army garrison is bivouacked on the edge of the town as part of the full-blown occupation of Kurdistan.

Within a few years, this relocation program will have drastically changed the culture of Kurdistan, which has always been marked by open lines of communication between clans across international borders. One young Kurd told visiting reporters that "we don't want to lose touch with each other"—a central reason for the Kurdish rebellion, but only one. The Kurds also want greater autonomy and a share of the mineral wealth under Kurdish lands.

During the war with Iran, Kurdish rebel leaders Massoud Barzani and Jalal Talabani saw a chance to gain advantage against Baghdad by siding with Tehran, even leading Revolutionary Guards into Iraqi Kurdistan for surprise attacks. But when the Iraqi Army went on the offensive last May, Iran's armed forces broke and the Kurdish rebellion collapsed.

Military Attacks

What happened afterward still is being pieced together by the West, but the best reconstruction available from western and

Asian diplomats suggests that Iraq mobilized 40,000 to 60,000 troops for an assault on and occupation of the remote valleys of Kurdistan, which had been ceded to the rebels during the last years of the war.

On Aug. 3–4, the Iraqi army may have air dropped some chemical weapons on Barzani and Talabani bases, setting off a general panic that quickly spread through the region. Iraqi troops may have hoped to execute a "pincer" movement to seal the northern border and then sweep up from the south to surround and wipe out the 20,000 rebel fighters.

As one western ambassador in Baghdad said, "If they had successfully kept them in Iraq, they could have done what they like without the world knowing about it."

Instead, many of the rebels and perhaps more than 100,000 civilian refugees fled into Turkey and Iran. Alarms immediately went off in western capitals and human-rights institutions. "The Iraqis were forced to stop that action," said one official from a regional government involved in the crisis.

What remains unknown is how many guerrillas were trapped by the Iraqi army and killed in the intense assault on rebel bases that occurred between Aug. 27 and Sept. 5.

"It could be thousands," said one diplomat.

Batufa was spared. The rebels did not live here. So this stop on our aerial tour has proved nothing, except that the people here are still alive, as they are in the other cities and towns of Kurdistan.

They are living in a real world, where nations struggling for national survival may practice revenge on a brutal scale.

When that happens, people may raise the alarm of "genocide" to stop the brutality, even when the term does not apply.

The Kurds Should Be Granted an Independent State

Namo Abdullah

In the following viewpoint, a Kurdish journalist living in Iraq reports on the Kurds' growing voice for a more autonomous and independent state. With the birth of the new African nation, South Sudan, comes a great deal of inspiration for the Kurds, he says. He argues that other recent events—such as the fall of Saddam Hussein, Turkey's desire to join the European Union, and the pro-democracy uprising in Syria—may significantly alter the outlook for a Kurdish state. Namo Abdullah is a recent graduate of the Columbia University Graduate School of Journalism who has been published in the New York Times, *Islam Online, and the* Human Rights Tribune. *This article is from the* Daily Star, *a leading English-language newspaper in Lebanon.*

On the day the newest African nation, South Sudan, was born, Iraqi Kurdish leader Barham Salih tweeted his feelings to the world on his iPad: "Watching history in [the] making as South Sudan goes independent . . . the [moral] of [the] story, right to self-determination cannot be denied by genocide.

Thousands of Kurds demonstrate in Khanaqin, Iraq, to demand the right to raise the Kurdish region's flag over government buildings. © AP Images.

"With the emergence of a new nation in Africa and uprisings against autocracies across the Arab world, Kurds in Iraq's semi-autonomous north are speaking in louder voices about the possibility of increasing autonomy if, as some Kurds fear, Iraq's central government becomes more authoritarian.

In parts of Turkey, Syria and Iran, Kurds are also seeing new possibilities of freedom beyond governments who have historically repressed their Kurdish minorities.

"There is a lot of inspiration from Southern Sudan," said Salih, prime minister of Iraqi Kurdistan, where Kurdish flags and colors—red, white and green—are far more common than the red, white and black of Iraq.

"But more important is the deep concern that most of us feel about the direction of the politics of Baghdad as it goes towards more centralization and authoritarianism."

ESTIMATES OF KURDISH POPULATION, 2011	
Country	**Estimate**
Turkey	12–14 million, about 18 percent of the population (although some estimates go up to 23 percent)
Iran	6–7 million, about 10 percent of the population
Iraq	5.5–6 million, about 20 percent of the population
Syria	1–1.5 million, about 7 percent of the population
Europe	1.5 million (an estimated 500,000 to 800,000 reside in Germany)
Caucasus	300,000 (Armenia = 1.8 percent of population, Azerbaijan = 2.5 percent of population, and Georgia = less than 1 percent of population)
Lebanon	up to 100,000
Israel	up to 100,000
Total	26–30 million

Taken from: Vera Eccarius-Kelly, *The Militant Kurds: A Dual Strategy for Freedom*. Santa Barbara, CA: Praeger, 2011, p. 203.

Iraq's central government and the Kurdish region—three of Iraq's 18 provinces—have unresolved issues over borders and oil rights. Iraqi Kurdistan has 45 billion barrels of crude reserves.

With a population of about 30 million, largely living in Iraq, Iran, Syria and Turkey, Kurds are an ethnic group whose culture and language separate them from Arabs, Turks and Persians, with whom they share land.

After the first Gulf war in 1991 Western powers provided a safe haven for Iraq's Kurds, allowing them to use their natural resources to start building a modern state.

Reinforced Notions of Kurdish Nationalism

Notions of Kurdish nationalism were reinforced by the 2003 invasion that toppled dictator Saddam Hussein as much of Iraq tumbled into sectarian warfare that threatened its survival as a single state.

"For the first time in their modern history, the Kurds in Iraq and Turkey, at least, are cautiously ascending," said author Michael Gunter, who has written on the evolution of Kurds in the two countries.

He said Turkey's desire to join the European Union has forced Turkey to improve Kurdish lives in the southeast. Kurdish music is heard in Turkish cities such as Diyarbakir, and a Kurdish-language TV channel broadcasts round-the-clock.

After 27 years of conflict between Turkey and Kurdish rebels, both Kurds and Turks appear to prefer more peaceful solutions to end the hostility. Turkish Prime Minister Recep Tayyip Erdogan has acknowledged the existence of a Kurdish problem, long denied as a "security issue," and promised to solve it. In June elections, Kurds won 36 parliamentary seats, almost double their previous total.

From the streets of Syria's Qamishli, where Kurdish protesters call for freedom, to the Citadel in Irbil, where a Kurdish flag waves over Iraq's biggest boomtown, many Kurds see a promising future for pan-Kurdish nationalism.

"There is no such a thing as half-revolution," said Khalid Ali, a Syrian Kurdish activist in Irbil.

"Syrians have decided it. The toppling of Bashar Assad is just matter of time," he said, referring to the Syrian leader who has cracked down on pro-democracy protests. Syria blames armed groups linked to Islamists for stirring violence.

Fall of Syrian Regime Is Good News for the Kurds

Exiled Syrian activists living in Iraqi Kurdistan are using social media tools such as Facebook, and collect donated money to support protesters at home.

"If this regime falls, it would be better for the Kurds. They will be free to work in their own regions," said Mahmoud Yaaqub, 34, who administers Facebook groups in Irbil.

David Romano, a Middle East politics professor at Missouri State University, says the success of the Syrian revolution would have profound impact on other countries, including Iran.

"Iran will be more isolated if Syria falls," said Romano, the author of *The Kurdish Nationalist Movement.*

From a hideout in the Qandil Mountains, Amir Karimi, a senior anti-Iran rebel leader, offers a different vision.

"If Syria falls, Iran would be the next target," he said. "Turkey would be left with two choices: Either to wipe out the Kurds completely . . . or surrender to reality."

It Is Too Risky to Set Up an Independent State for the Kurds

David Romano

In the following viewpoint, an American journalist and professor argues that all Kurds in Iraq would like independence. He says that this is reasonable given their history of oppression at the hands of the Iraqi government. However, he contends that since the fall of Saddam Hussein in 2003, Kurds in Iraq have had a good deal of autonomy and appear to be thriving. He maintains that the Kurds know that a push for independence would result in bloody reprisals, not only from the Iraqi central government, but from neighboring states that have no desire for an independent Kurdistan. He reports that given the risks, Iraqi Kurds are therefore willing to wait for independence. David Romano teaches international studies at Rhodes College and is the author of The Kurdish Nationalist Movement.

One of Iraq's worst kept secrets is that Iraqi Kurds want an independent state. Whitehall [that is, the British government] included the Kurds of what was then the Mosul vilayet (province) of the Ottoman Empire into its newly crafted Iraq some 80 years ago and for most of that time the forced marriage has not been a happy one.

Hoping for Independence

During my first visit to the Kurdish autonomous region of Iraq, in the summer of 1994, the area was in the throes of a full blown civil war. The 1991 Gulf War had allowed Iraq's Kurds the opportunity to run their own affairs for the first time, in a safe haven the size of Switzerland established by the U.S., Britain and France. But the two main Iraqi Kurdish parties—the Kurdistan Democratic Party (KDP) and the Patriotic Union of Kurdistan (PUK)—had begun fighting over the scraps of smuggling revenue that consisted of the near-destitute safe haven's main source of income. Also suffering from double sanctions (the international ones placed on Iraq and Saddam's sanctions against the Iraqi Kurdish region) and unfriendly regimes in every direction—in Baghdad [Iraq], Damascus [Syria], Teheran [Iran] and Ankara [Turkey]—the future did not look bright.

Despite this, every Kurd I spoke to was thrilled to be free of Baghdad's grip, however tenuously. With their history of central government neglect, repression, deportations, forced assimilation and finally chemical weapon-borne genocide in 1988, it is not hard to see why.

I travelled to Iraqi Kurdistan again in the autumn of 2000, and then lived there for just short of a year in 2003 and 2004. Still, I have yet to meet an Iraqi Kurd who does not favour an independent Kurdistan. For most Kurds I spoke to, the question was "when" rather than "if" they would have an independent state. The answer, however, was "not right now, but hopefully within the next 50 years."

For Kurds, Iraq's territorial integrity is not some sacred value that trumps their right to self-determination. The lives of thousands, even hundreds of thousands, of their people are sacred. A push for Iraqi Kurdish statehood in today's Middle Eastern context would put that many lives at risk. In addition to mainly Arab Iraq, Turkey, Iran and Syria all have significant Kurdish minorities of their own, chafing under central government rule, and these states would harshly oppose such a move lest it set

Cadets stand next to a photo of Jalal Talabani, who was elected as the first Kurdish president of Iraq in 2005. © Ed Kashi/Corbis.

a precedent for their own Kurdish citizens. The armies of these neighbouring states might intervene quickly to assist Baghdad in re-establishing control of Iraqi Kurdistan, or to try and claim chunks of territory for themselves.

Even if they managed to secede with Kirkuk [a city in northeast Iraq, near or in Iraqi Kurdistan] and its significant oil reserves, landlocked Iraqi Kurds would still need to transport their oil to foreign markets, either via tanker trucks or pipelines. Surrounded by unfriendly regimes, they would be cut off from the world and placed in an economic and political choke hold.

Gaining Ground

Autonomous Iraqi Kurdistan has made some impressive gains since 1991, and even more since Saddam's overthrow in 2003. The region went from being Iraq's poorest and least developed historically to its richest, and the Kurdistan Regional Government actively courts investors and even tourists with ad campaigns such as theotheriraq.com.

Construction cranes dominate the skylines of Iraqi Kurdish cities like Erbil, Suleimaniya and Duhok, with Turkish investors accounting for some 80 percent of business. The KDP and PUK have buried their animosity and are nearly finished unifying into one Kurdish regional administration. Kurds also now play a prominent role in Iraq's central government, holding the Presidency (Jalal Talabani), Foreign Ministry (Hoshyar Zebari) and one of the Vice-Prime Minister positions (Barham Salih).

All this would be put at risk by a hasty bid for statehood. Nor do Iraqi Kurds wish to risk their present gains by supporting or stoking Kurdish unrest amongst Syrian, Turkish and Iranian Kurds. The Iraqi Kurdish bid to control extra territory in Iraq, especially oil-rich Kirkuk and parts of Diyala province, is also probably not an attempt to seed the ground for secession in the near future. In any case, the Iraqi constitution requires them to turn over revenues from all existing oil fields to Baghdad for proportional distribution amongst all Iraqis.

Rather, they simply want to include most of Iraq's Kurds in the autonomous Kurdish region. Of course, physically controlling some one third of Iraq's oil fields might also go a long way towards making sure that the government in Baghdad actually shares the revenues amongst all Iraqis, which is not a bad idea given the country's previous history.

Although a complete accommodation breakdown in Baghdad between Kurds and Arabs might push them towards riskier choices, for the foreseeable future Iraq's Kurds therefore appear content with the fruits of autonomy. If 40 to 50 years from now the Middle East and the world appears ready for a Kurdish state, they will be too.

The United States Has Nobly Protected Weaker Nations and Groups Like the Kurds

Victor Davis Hanson

In the following viewpoint, a military historian argues that the United States has long protected weak nations and peoples, such as Taiwan, the Kurds, Greece, and Israel. He says that these nations are surrounded by enemies, and without US help, many of them would disappear. He concedes that it is tempting to abandon such allies since they can be difficult and offer the United States few strategic advantages. However, he concludes that the United States should continue to protect the weak, because doing so is central to US values. Victor Davis Hanson is a frequent writer for National Review *and the author of* The Father of Us All: War and History, Ancient and Modern.

Recently, an open mike caught French president Nicolas Sarkozy and American president Barack Obama jointly trashing Israeli prime minister Benjamin Netanyahu. Sarkozy scoffed, "I cannot stand him. He's a liar."

Obama trumped that with, "You're fed up with him, but I have to deal with him every day."

Victor Davis Hanson, "Why Does America Defend the Weak and Small?," *National Review*, November 17, 2011. Copyright © 2011 by National Review. All rights reserved. Reproduced by permission.

Saving the Weak

Two days later, in one of the most bizarre op-eds published by the *New York Times* in recent memory, Paul Kane suggested that the United States could literally sell out its support for democratic Taiwan for about $1 trillion. He argued that the Chinese might be so thankful to us for letting them get their hands on the island that they might forgive much of what we owe them.

So why does the United States take risks in guaranteeing the security of countries such as Israel and Taiwan? Surely the smart money—and most of the world—bets on their richer enemies. The Arab Middle East has oil, hundreds of millions of people, and lots of dangerous radical-Islamic terrorists. China is more than one billion strong, with the fastest-growing economy in the world.

But President Obama should remember that America does not think solely in terms of national advantage. In fact, only the United States seems to have an affinity for protecting tiny, vulnerable nations. In two wars, and more than twelve years of no-fly zones in Iraq, America saved the Kurds from a genocidal Saddam Hussein.

Greece today has few friends. Its northern-European creditors are furious with its profligacy and duplicity. Nearby, an ascendant Turkey is flexing its muscles over occupied Cyprus and new finds of gas and oil in the Aegean and eastern Mediterranean. In short, a bankrupt Greece of only 11 million people, residing in one of history's most dangerous neighborhoods, has few strong friends other than the United States. The same is true of Christian Armenia, which likewise is relatively small and near to historical enemies in Turkey and Russia.

All of these peoples—Israelis, anti-Communist Chinese, Kurds, Greeks, and Armenians—have a few things in common. They have relatively small—and often shrinking—populations, aggressive neighbors, few strong allies, many expatriates and refugees in the United States, and tragic histories of persecution and genocide. Half the world's Jews were lost to the Holocaust.

"...IN OTHER NEWS, A KURDISH GROUP TODAY ANNOUNCED PLANS TO SEND HUMANITARIAN AID TO BRITISH AND AMERICAN TAXPAYERS...."

"In other news, a Kurdish group today announced plans to send humanitarian aid to British and American taxpayers . . . ," cartoon by Rex May ("Baloo"), www.CartoonStock .com. Copyright © by Rex May ("Baloo"). Reproduction rights obtainable from www .CartoonStock.com.

Had Mao Tse-tung [the first leader of Communist China]—the most prolific mass murderer in history—gotten his way, the entire anti-Communist Chinese population who fled in terror to Taiwan [in 1949] would have been wiped out. In the early 1920s, nearly a million Greeks perished in Asia Minor—ethnically cleansed by a Turkey that had at one time conquered and occupied Greece for more than 350 years. A million Armenians perished in the breakup of the Ottoman Empire during World War I. The stateless Kurds have often been persecuted by Arabs, Iranians, and Turks.

The Values of the United States
We should remember that in the late 1940s Greece and Taiwan would have disappeared as free, independent countries without

American military support and guarantees. Armenia did not exist as a free nation until America helped to force the collapse of the Soviet Union [in 1991]. Kurdistan emerged as an autonomous province only when America deposed Saddam Hussein [in 2003]. Israel might have vanished during the 1973 Yom Kippur War without massive American military aid.

Of course, these historically persecuted peoples can at times be testy allies, and they can even sound anti-American. Their national characters—reflecting centuries of oppression—understandably can seem prone to collective paranoia and conspiracy theories. Yet Israel, Taiwan, Kurdistan, Greece, and Armenia are democratic states, with rich histories, and have survived against all odds.

In the next few years, as never before, our small friends will be tested. Iran has promised to wipe out Israel and may soon get the bomb to do it. We are withdrawing all troops at the end of the year from Iraq, and Kurdistan will then be entirely on its own. Russia often talks about reconstituting its former Soviet states into some sort of new imperial federation. China thinks it is only a matter of time before Taiwan can be absorbed. The new Turkey is beginning to look a lot like the old imperial Ottoman sultanate.

Yet if protecting these small states is risky, our concern also reflects positively upon the singular values of the United States. The United Nations has neither the will nor the capability to ensure the security of these countries. The eroding European Union talks grandly of international values but rarely risks its blood or treasure to defend them.

Only America is moral enough and strong enough to protect the world's historically vulnerable but culturally unique peoples. It would be a shame if we forgot that—either out of desire for profit or because we became fed up with the bother.

Chapter Three: Saddam Hussein's American Train

Larry Everest

In the following viewpoint, an American journalist argues that the United States has often justified intervention in Iraq and the Middle East by claiming to be fighting for Kurdish rights. However, the United States has repeatedly betrayed the Kurds, he says. In particular, he points to events in the 1970s, when the United States and Iran funded a Kurdish rebellion against Iraq. The United States never intended the Kurds to actually obtain autonomy, according to the author. After concessions were obtained from Iraq, the United States abandoned the Kurds without warning, facilitating a brutal repression on the part of Iraq. Larry Everest reports on the Middle East and Central Asia, and his work has appeared in many newspapers, including Revolutionary Worker, Boston Globe, *and the* Los Angeles Times. *This viewpoint is an excerpt from his 2004 book,* Oil, Power and Empire: Iraq and the US Global Agenda.

Playing the Kurdish "Card" (Again!)

To hear the Bush II administration tell it, Iraq's Kurds could have no better allies than their self-proclaimed friends in Washington.

Larry Everest, "Chapter Three: Sadaam Hussein's American Train," *Oil, Power and Empire: Iraq and the US Global Agenda*. Monroe, ME: Common Courage Press, 2004, pp. 79–84. Copyright © 2004 by Common Courage Press. All rights reserved. Reproduced by permission.

Bush and company repeatedly denounced the Hussein regime's "persecution of its civilian population, including Shi'a, Sunnis, Kurds, Turkomans and others," as Bush put it before the United Nations in September 2002, and argued that war, conquest, and regime change were needed to assure Kurdish freedoms.[97]

The proponents of the 2003 war never saw fit, of course, to mention the actual, sordid record of Washington's manipulation and betrayal of the Kurds during the 1970s, which we delve into below. That history not only makes U.S. promises ring hollow and hypocritical, but casts Washington's true intentions toward the Kurds in a starkly different light.

In 1972, Nixon, Kissinger and Iran's Shah also came up with a cynical plan to deal with its concerns in the Persian Gulf: encouraging an insurgency by Iraq's Kurds in order to weaken Baghdad. In May, Nixon and Kissinger visited Moscow and promised that the U.S. would join the Soviets to "promote conditions in which all countries will live in peace and security and will not be subject to outside interference." Seymour Hersh, a long-time investigative journalist for the *New York Times* and later the *New Yorker*, writes in his biography of Kissinger that, "The next day, Nixon and Kissinger flew to Tehran and made a secret commitment to the Shah to clandestinely supply arms to the Kurdish rebel faction inside Soviet-supported Iraq...."[98] The goal, Kissinger later explained, was for the Shah to "keep Iraq occupied by supporting the Kurdish rebellion within Iraq, and maintain a large army near the frontier."[99]

Since Iraq's creation by the British, its Kurdish population has suffered systematic discrimination and oppression. Much of Iraq's oil flows from fields around Kirkuk in Iraqi Kurdistan. Yet Iraqi Kurds saw few benefits from Iraq's petroleum wealth and had no voice in its oil policy. Kurdistan remained undeveloped, with fewer industries, roads, schools, and hospitals than the rest of Iraq. Kurds were discriminated against in government employment and had little control over even their local affairs.

Following the Ba'ath takeover in 1968, the new regime promised Kurds that their lot would improve. Iraq's new 1970 constitution recognized "the national rights of the Kurdish People and the legitimate rights of all minorities within the unity of Iraq." A 1974 "Law for Autonomy in the Area of Kurdistan" promised that Kurdish would be an official language, used in Kurdish schools.[100] These actions marked Iraq's broadest official recognition of Kurdish identity and rights. (In contrast, neighboring Iran and Turkey, then staunch U.S. allies, have never even formally recognized the Kurds as a distinct nationality, let alone promised them national rights.)

However, during negotiations in 1971 between the Ba'ath regime and Kurdish representatives, it became clear that the key issues of Kurdish control of local security forces, receiving a fair portion of Iraq's oil income, and sharing national power were not on the table. The Ba'ath also began encouraging Iraqi Arabs to move to Kurdistan and attempted to assassinate Kurdish leader Mustafa Barzani. Barzani, who had been in contact with the U.S. and the Shah (and perhaps Israel) since the early 1960s, turned to them once again for help against Baghdad.[101] Barzani even promised the *Washington Post* that if the U.S. backed the Kurdish struggle, "we are ready to do what goes with American policy in this area if America will protect us from the wolves. If support were strong enough, we could control the Kirkuk field and give it to an American company to operate."[102]

The Kissinger-Shah plan went into effect in 1972. Iran and the U.S. encouraged the Kurds to rise against Baghdad and provided them millions of dollars in weapons, logistical support, and funds. Over the next 3 years, $16 million in CIA money was given to Iraq's Kurds, and Iran provided the Kurds with some 90 percent of their weapons, including advanced artillery.[103]

The U.S. goal, however, was neither victory nor self-determination for Iraqi Kurds. The CIA feared such a strategy "would have the effect of prolonging the insurgency, thereby encouraging separatist aspirations and possibly providing to the

Soviet Union an opportunity to create difficulties" for U.S. allies Turkey and Iran.[104] A Congressional investigation of CIA activities, headed by New York Congressman Otis Pike, concluded that "none of the nations who were aiding [the Kurds] seriously desired that they realize their objective of an autonomous state."[105] Rather, the U.S. and the Shah sought to weaken Iraq and deplete its energies. According to CIA memos and cables, they viewed the Kurds as "a card to play" against Iraq, and "a uniquely useful tool for weakening [Iraq's] potential for international adventurism."

To this end, Iran instituted "draconian controls" on its military assistance and never gave the Kurds more than three days worth of ammunition in order to deny them the freedom of action needed for victory.[106] At one point in 1973, Kissinger personally intervened to halt a planned Kurdish offensive for fear it would succeed and complicate U.S. machinations in the wake of the October Arab-Israeli War.[107] The Pike investigation concluded:

> The president, Dr. Kissinger, and the Shah hoped that our clients would not prevail. They preferred instead that the insurgents simply continue a level of hostilities sufficient to sap the resources of our ally's [Iran's] neighbouring country. The policy was not imparted to our clients, who were encouraged to continue fighting.[108]

"Ours Was a Cynical Enterprise"

By 1975, the Kurdish insurgency posed the gravest threat the Ba'ath Regime had yet faced. Some 45,000 Kurdish guerrillas, aided by two Iranian divisions, had pinned down 80 percent of Iraq's 100,000 troops, severely straining Iraq's economy and military.[109] Kissinger and the Shah wanted neither all-out war, nor the collapse of the Iraqi regime. Rather, they sought to force Iraq to curb its anti-Israeli Arab nationalism and to pry it from its Soviet patrons, demonstrating to others in the region that being a Soviet client didn't pay. The Shah also wanted to prove that Iran

Kurdish rebels camp at Khree Neozang, Iraq, home to the Patriotic Union of Kurdistan (PUK) guerrillas, in 1979. The Kurds have felt betrayed and abandoned by the United States in their quest to gain independence from Iraq. © Christian Simonpietri/Sygma/Corbis.

was the Gulf's strongest power and a reliable regional gendarme for the U.S., as well as to renegotiate the Sa'dabad Pact of 1937, which had given control of the entire Shatt al Arab waterway between the two countries to Iraq.[110]

The Shah planned to abandon the Kurds "the minute he came to an agreement with his enemy over border disputes," one CIA memo noted. Eight hours after Iraq did agree to U.S.-Iranian terms, which were formalized in the Algiers Agreement of March 1975, the Shah and the U.S. cut off aid—including food—and closed Iran's border, cutting off Kurdish lines of retreat.[111]

The Kurds had no idea that they were about to be abandoned. But Iraq knew, and the next day it launched an all-out, "search-and-destroy" attack. The Kurds, who had been led to believe that the U.S. was acting as a "guarantor" against betrayal by the Shah, were taken by complete surprise. Deprived of Iranian support, Kurdish forces were quickly decimated and between 150,000 and 300,000 Kurds were forced to flee into Iran.[112]

The U.S. coldly betrayed its erstwhile Kurdish "allies," but even then, as the Pike Commission sardonically noted, "The cynicism of the U.S. and its ally had not yet completely run its course." Barzani had written to Kissinger, pleading desperately for help. Kissinger didn't bother replying.

Washington then "refused to extend humanitarian assistance to the thousands of refugees created by the abrupt termination of military aid," the Pike Commission reported. One CIA cable acknowledged, "[O]ur ally [Iran] was later to forcibly return over 40,000 of the refugees and the United States government refused to admit even one refugee into the United States by way of political asylum even though they qualified for such admittance."[113]

The U.S.-Iranian covert campaign further poisoned relations between Baghdad and Iraq's Kurds. The Pike Commission concluded that if the U.S. and the Shah hadn't encouraged the insurgency, the Kurds "may have reached an accommodation with the central government, thus gaining at least a measure of autonomy while avoiding further bloodshed. Instead, our clients [the Kurds] fought on, sustaining thousands of casualties and 200,000 refugees."[114]

Baghdad also retaliated with a massive pacification campaign: some 250,000 Kurds were forcibly relocated to central and southern Iraq, while many Arab Iraqis were forced to move to into traditionally Kurdish areas.[115]

In what became an infamous remark, Kissinger dismissed the Pike Commission's concerns: "Covert action," he said, "should not be confused with missionary work." Nonetheless, the Commission concluded, "Even in this context of covert operations, ours was a cynical enterprise."[116] It is important to note here that as these events were taking place (beginning in September 1973), Kissinger's top aide was General Brent Scowcroft, who would later become National Security Advisor under Bush, Sr.

and an architect of the 1991 Persian Gulf war on Iraq. It is also important to note that if the U.S. government had had its way, the Pike Commission's damning exposures would have never seen the light of day. First, the House of Representatives voted not to release the document. The, when CBS correspondent Daniel Schorr obtained a leaked copy and gave it to the *Village Voice*, he was promptly fired by CBS and threatened with contempt of Congress for refusing to reveal his sources. A new Director of Central Intelligence had just been appointed when this attempted cover-up took place. His name was George H.W. Bush.[117]

As we'll explore in the next chapter, the United States government again resorted to a cynical "no win" strategy during the Iran-Iraq war of the 1980s with even more horrific consequences for Iranians, Iraqis and Kurds.

References

97. Bush, *Wall Street Journal*, September 12, 2002.
98. Seymour M. Hersh, The Price of Power: Kissinger in the Nixon White House (New York: Summit Books, 1983), 542
99. Kissinger, Years of Upheaval, 674-75
100. Middle East Watch, 70
101. Tripp, 200-201
102. Dinsmore, Washington Report on Middle East Affaris, May/June 1991; *Washington Post*, June 22, 1973 cited in Simons, 302
103. Bulloch and Morris, No Friends But the Mountains, 138-39
104. CIA: The Pike Report (United Kingdom: Spokesman Books, 1977), 211. Extensive excerpts from the select Committee on Intelligence, or Pike report, were also published in the *New York Times* and the *Village Voice*. "The CIA Report the President Doesn't Want You to Read," *Village Voice*, February 16, 1976; "House Committee Finds Intelligence Agencies Generally Go Unchecked" and "Intelligence Report Leaks Denounced by White House," articles by Nicholas M. Horrock and John M. Crewdson, *New York Times*, January 26 and 27, 1976.
105. Pike Report, 214
106. Vanly, 187
107. Bulloch and Morris, No Friends But the Mountains, 140
108. Pike Report, 197
109. Dilip Hiro, The Longest War (New York: Routledge, 1991), 16; Simons, 303
110. Vanly, 186
111. Vanly, 187
112. Pike Report 197-98; Cleveland, 398-99; Vanly, 189
113. Pike Report, 198, 217
114. Pike Report, 197

115. Cleveland, 398-99
116. Pike Report, 197
117. Otis Pike, "We've Given Them False Hope Before," *San Francisco Examiner*, April 10, 1991; Daniel Schorr, "1975 Background to Betrayal," *Washington Post*, April 7, 1991, D3; Christopher Hitchens, "Minority Report," *The Nation*, May 6, 1991, 58; all cited in Tony Murphy, "Encouraging Rebellion: The Cynical Use of the Kurds and the Shiites," in "High Crimes and Misdemeanors: U.S. War Crimes in the Persian Gulf," Research Committee of the San Francisco Commission of Inquiry of the International War Crimes Tribunal, 1991

Iraqi Arabs Flock to Kurdistan

Yahya Barzanji and Karin Laub

In the following viewpoint, the authors argue that Kurdistan is peaceful and economically thriving after the fall of Saddam Hussein. They report that it has been a good season for souvenir shops and hotels in Kurdistan. In the days of Saddam, even Kurdistan was largely off-limits for Iraqis. Now, the Iraqi government actually encourages tourism to the Kurdistan region and that has improved the economy there. Yahya Barzanji and Karin Laub are writers based in the Middle East and contributors to AP Worldstream.

Iraqis can finally get away from it all.

After five years of war and sectarian bloodshed, they have been able to travel to the green, tranquil mountains of northern Iraq's Kurdistan region by the thousands this summer, leaving behind the heat, dust and daily killings in their country's heartland.

Organized bus tours to autonomous Kurdistan are made possible by improved security in recent months, though roads remain treacherous and visitors are stopped at a string of roadblocks before reaching their vacation getaways.

Students practice on looms at the textile museum in Erbil, the capital city of Iraqi Kurdistan. The area has emerged from the devastation of war to become an investment hub and tourist destination. © Sebastian Meyer/Corbis.

More than 23,000 Iraqis headed to Kurdistan this summer, up from 3,700 last year, tourism officials say. A week in a modest hotel, with bus fare, costs about US$160 per person, or one-third an average monthly salary.

Still, it's been a good season for Kurdish hotel and souvenir shop owners.

And the budding tourist trade is helping to soften some of the hard feelings between Iraq's Kurdish minority and Arab majority.

The two share a bloody history, particularly Saddam Hussein's brutal repression of the Kurds and establishment of their U.S.-protected self-ruled region in 1991.

Since the fall of Saddam in 2003, Kurds have held key positions in the national government, including the presidency. The

Kurdish region has also absorbed thousands of displaced Arab families and workers, Kurdish officials say.

Now, with large numbers of Iraqi Arabs trekking north for vacation, more and more ordinary people are getting to know each other in a peaceful setting.

"I have no resentment against Arabs who come to Kurdistan as workers or tourists," said Hama Rashid, 47, who translates political books into Arabic, Turkish and Persian and as a young man fought Saddam's soldiers as a member of the Kurdish Peshmerga forces.

"We want Kurdistan to be the touristic destination for Arabs who will pump money into our economy," Rashid said.

Mazin Zidan, visiting Sulaimaniyah from chaotic Baghdad, about 160 miles (260 kilometers) away, said he was impressed by the orderly traffic and friendly police in Kurdistan. "All my bad impressions about the Kurds have been wiped out," said Zidan, 28, strolling in the city's Freedom Park, once site of an Iraqi army base where Kurds were imprisoned.

Zidan said he was reluctant at first to make the trip, unsure of how he would be received.

There are tensions between the Kurds and the central government, particularly over the fate of Kirkuk, an ethnically mixed city just south of Kurdistan claimed by the Kurds.

Nevertheless, the Iraqi government and the authorities in Kurdistan, comprising three of Iraq's 18 provinces, have encouraged the bus convoys. The Iraqi and Kurdish tourism ministers met in March and licensed 38 travel agents to arrange the Kurdistan tours, said Abdul-Zahra Talakani, spokesman for the ministry in Baghdad.

For the Kurds, it's mainly business. For the central government, it may also be politics.

"Kurdistan is part of Iraq, and we encourage Iraqis living in the south and center to visit the Kurdish region," Tourism Minister Kahtan Abbas said in an interview.

Talakani's small office, stuffed with clunky computers and files stacked against a wall, has a lone tourism poster on the wall—showing a lush landscape in the Kurdish city of Irbil, referred to by its Kurdish name, Hawler.

Iraq's Kurdistan, about the size of Switzerland and home to nearly 3.8 million people, is perhaps the only destination for Iraqis thirsting for a little normalcy.

Arab countries, trying to keep out Iraq's troubles, grant few visas, while Europe and the U.S. are too expensive for most. Iran is more welcoming, but largely attracts Shiite pilgrims.

During Saddam's rule, Iraqis were even more boxed in, with most barred from travel abroad.

In Saddam's days, even Kurdistan was largely off limits. The Kurds separated from the rest of Iraq after rising up against Saddam in 1991, aided by a U.S.-British no-fly zone that helped keep the dictator at bay.

After his 2003 ouster, Kurds eased border controls, leading to a first surge of Arab tourism that year, but closed the gates again in February 2004 when suicide bombers killed 109 people in an attack on Kurdish party offices.

Arab visitors are still carefully screened.

Kurdish troops board buses carrying Iraqi Arabs at checkpoints, and compare names with lists sent ahead by the travel agents, travelers say.

"We have very tight security. We don't want Sulaimaniyah to be like Fallujah," said Mohammed Ihsan, Kurdish minister of extra-regional affairs, referring to what was once Iraq's most violent city. "But the visitors are welcomed everywhere in Kurdistan."

The Kurdish Tourism Ministry says it hopes to double the number of Arab visitors next year.

The influx has been good for Sulaimaniyah.

Shamal Hama Ali, who owns the 25-room Mawlai hotel in the city, said more than half his guests are Arabs. Souvenir shop owner Saman Karim said his Arab customers favor items not easily available at home, such as crystal glasses and copies of classic paintings.

The visitors fill local restaurants, take their children to amusement parks or head out to small mountain resorts.

The Kurds and the central government also try to attract foreigners.

Several foreign airlines fly to Irbil and Sulaimaniyah, and the Kurdish government's web site boasts that not a single foreigner has been killed or kidnapped in its territory since 2003. Iranian pilgrims make up the bulk of the visitors to the rest of Iraq.

But tourism remains a high-risk business, and the Kurds could close their borders if sectarian violence flares again.

"Tourism is like a flower," said Talakani, the ministry spokesman. "It needs a good environment to flourish."

Kurdistan After Saddam Hussein Is Still Dependent on Foreign Support

Denise Natali, Henri J. Barkey, and Marina Ottaway

In the following viewpoint, the authors argue that, while Kurdistan is growing and prospering in some ways, it is still very dependent on aid from foreign donors and especially from the central government of Baghdad. The authors also argue that Kurdish political power in Iraq is wavering. They conclude that the success and stability of Iraqi Kurdistan are uncertain. Denise Natali is the research centers director at the American University of Iraq-Sulaimaniya; Henri J. Barkey and Marina Ottaway are both scholars at the Carnegie Endowment for International Peace.

Since the American occupation of Iraq began [in 2003], the Kurdistan Regional Government has enjoyed an unprecedented degree of autonomy. Kurdistan's economy has benefited from improvements in Iraq's domestic security situation, and international observers have suggested that this "quasi-state" is more prosperous and independent than ever before.

But despite the appearance of increasing autonomy, Kurdistan continues to rely heavily on the central Iraqi government and international support. This dependency has curtailed Kurdistan's separatist aspirations that have historically driven its negotiations with Baghdad. Denise Natali, the Research Centers Director at the American University of Iraq-Sulaimaniya and author of *The Kurdish Quasi-State*, and Carnegie's Henri J. Barkey discussed the current challenges facing Kurdistan as it struggles to maintain political leverage in the context of a fragmented Iraqi government. Carnegie's Marina Ottaway moderated the discussion.

Challenging the Myth of a "Booming" Kurdistan

In 2007, Kurdistan's two major parties, the Patriotic Union of Kurdistan (PUK) and the Kurdistan Democratic Party (KDP), decided to form a unified Kurdistan Regional Government (KRG). This union simplified the regional decision-making process and paved the way for rapid economic development.

Despite visible indicators of growth—such as the flurry of recent construction and infrastructure projects—Kurdistan is not as self-sufficient as some observers claim. Natali explained how Kurdistan's political and economic autonomy is fundamentally constrained by its dependence on Baghdad.

- A historical pattern of dependency: Kurdistan's dependence on external actors is not a new phenomenon; Barkey noted that Kurds in the past and the Kurdish quasi-state have repeatedly made deals with international players to advance their own security interests. Following the first Gulf war and the creation of a safe haven in northern Iraq, Kurdistan became an object of external patronage as foreign donors funneled aid into the war-torn region. Still, the same international sanctions imposed on Iraq were imposed on Kurdistan in order to downplay regional divisions. During this period, foreign aid was deliberately limited to food and fuel handouts, in the hopes of dampening Kurdish separatist aspirations.

- Increasing autonomy: Kurdish autonomy was considerably enhanced by the ratification of a new Iraqi constitution in 2005, explained Natali. The document provided a legal basis for Kurdish claims to political rights, national revenues, and recognition as a semi-autonomous region. At this time, Kurdistan enjoyed unprecedented legitimacy in the international community. Whereas foreign donors had previously limited their contributions to NGOs [nongovernmental organizations], they began funneling direct aid to the Kurdish government itself.

- Shifting dependency: Despite gains in autonomy, Kurdistan continues to depend on external patronage—although the source of that patronage has shifted over time. Kurdistan today relies on Baghdad for as much as 95 percent of its budget. Natali argued that the apparent increase in Kurdish autonomy is largely illusory; the quasi-state's recent economic windfalls would evaporate without Baghdad's heavy patronage.

- Economic activity: Nevertheless, the Kurdistan Regional Government (KRG) has sought to diversify its economic base by engaging foreign energy companies to prospect in its territory. Disputes with Baghdad over the hydrocarbon law have hampered the activities of these companies.

Maintaining Kurdistan's Foothold in a Fragmented National Government

The Kurds were once considered "kingmakers" in Iraq, and following the elections of December 2005 they played a key role in consolidating Iraq's diverse national factions into a unified government. However, Natali explained that the results of the March 2010 parliamentary elections—in which Kurds lost one of their 58 seats while the total number of seats increased from 275 to 325—reveal a clear decline in Kurdish influence.

DONORS AND AMOUNTS COMMITTED TO KURDISTAN, IRAQ, THROUGH 2009	
Donor	Amount (USD)
Denmark	205,641
Norway	253,688
United Kingdom	259,434
United Nations Development Programme	1,030,361
Sweden	1,369,091
United Nations Development Programme, Thematic Trust Fund (funded by European Union)	2,215,316
Japan	45,873,540
World Bank	85,000,000
Korea	94,950,425
United Nations Development Group, Iraq Trust Fund	106,056,150
World Bank, Iraq Trust Fund	129,315,383
United States of America	723,138,786
Total	1,184,667,806

Taken from: Kurdistan Regional Government, Ministry of Planning, *Report on Donor Contributions to the Kurdistan Region*, June 2009, p. 10.

- The challenge of a fragmented government: The Iraqi parliament's failure to form a coalition government since the 2010 election has hindered the Kurdish coalition's ability to promote its interests in Baghdad. Natali argued that the fragmented state of Iraq's national government has increased the political vulnerability of the Kurdish coalition, which will be unable to leverage its bargaining power until a new parliament is seated.

- Seeking to preserve influence: In an effort to maintain a political foothold, the Kurdish coalition presented a list of nineteen conditions as prerequisites for its participation in a future governing coalition. Natali interpreted these conditions—including the preservation of a federal system and a constitutional provision aimed at resolving territorial disputes—as an expression of the Kurdish coalition's own insecurities and its desire to reverse the erosion of its political influence in Baghdad.

- Beyond parliament: Although the Kurds have suffered a setback in their numerical representation in parliament, they continue to derive some political power from Iraq's institutional and legal framework. Under Iraq's power-sharing arrangement, the Kurdish leader Jalal Talabani serves as president of the country. Barkey contended that Talabani enjoys greater legitimacy in the international community than either former Prime Minister Ayyad Allawi or current Prime Minister Nouri al-Maliki. Through their command of key, symbolic posts, "the Kurds punch above their weight," Barkey said.

Because of its continuing dependence on external recognition and aid, Kurdistan's future trajectory is pegged to the fates of its various benefactors. Kurdistan's survival as a semi-autonomous entity will hinge on its ability to gain acceptance from the rest of Iraq's population and sustain a stable political relationship with Baghdad while maximizing its concessions from the central government. "The Kurdistan Regional Government is a process," Barkey said. "We do not know how it will turn out."

Kurdistan After Saddam Hussein Is a Violent Gangster State

Justin Raimondo

The author of the following reports on the arrest and imprison-ment of Kamal Said Qadir by the Kurdish government. He says that Qadir was arrested because he had written insulting articles about members of the Kurdish government. The Kurdish govern-ment is authoritarian and is rife with corruption, the author ar-gues. He claims that many Americans who supported the 2003 invasion of Iraq have tried to portray Kurdistan as thriving and successful in order to justify the invasion. In contrast, he concludes that Kurdistan is another aspect of the US failure in Iraq. Justin Raimondo is the editorial director of the website Antiwar.com.

Dr. Kamal Said Qadir, also known as Kamal Berzenji, was kidnapped by the agents of the Kurdish Democratic Party [KDP]'s intelligence unit, Parastin, on Oct. 26, 2005, and jailed. His "crime": writing "insulting" articles about Kurdish Democratic Party high mucky-muck and Kurdish Regional Government (KRG) President Massoud Barzani. In short, he committed *lese-majeste*, i.e., Qadir wounded the dignity of the king. After a "trial" that lasted one hour, he was sentenced to 30 years in prison.

Justin Raimondo, "Kurdistan: A Gangster State," Antiwar.com, January 10, 2006. Copyright © 2006 by Antiwar.com. All rights reserved. Reproduced by permission.

This is what the "liberation" of Iraq [through the 2003 U.S.-led invasion and the overthrow of Saddam Hussein] has accomplished.

Democracy, Iraq Style

Qadir was born in a small village south of Hawler in southern Kurdistan and immigrated to Austria in 1978, where he studied law at the Vienna Law School. A former university instructor in Sulemani and Hawler, he was forced to flee Kurdistan again— after the "liberation" by the Americans—because he demanded more human rights and democracy in southern Kurdistan. At the time of his kidnapping, he was engaged in research activities in the field of constitutional law at the Faculty of Law in Vienna. He returned in order to set up a human rights monitoring group and to pursue legal action against the Kurdish Democratic Party, promising to reveal the secrets of the Barzani crime family. En route to a meeting with KDP officials in Arbil, he was arrested by KDP intelligence agents. Dr. Qadir was, in other words, lured and entrapped.

Semi-official U.S. protests over his detainment are belied by the news that the Kurds are rounding up their internal political opponents—with the active assistance of U.S. military forces— and stashing them in secret jails. Qadir is now on a hunger strike, and his health is rapidly deteriorating.

The Kurdish authorities—who have launched an ethnic-cleansing campaign against Arabs and are now readying them-selves to seize the oil-rich city of Kirkuk, in northern Iraq—were doubtless enraged when Radio Free Europe cited Qadir in this piece about Kurdish corruption:

> Kamal Berzenji wrote in an article published by kurdishmedia .com in December 2002: "The members of the [Kurdish] secu-rity services . . . try to make a business out of their powers by accusing and arresting anybody whom they think they could blackmail and extract money from." He says the practice has its roots in Hussein's Ba'athist regime, but was also practiced

during the Kurdish civil war in the 1990s. "One of the reasons [for that war is] business—and profit-making by some Kurdish warlords on both sides. Some of them grew [into] millionaires by confiscating and stealing the property of his fellow Kurdish brothers."

It's as if reporters for the *Washington Post*, the *New York Times*, and other major media outlets were arrested for reporting on the buying of the Republican congressional caucus by Jack Abramoff & Co.[1] They don't dare do that in America—quite yet—but in Kurdistan, to speak out against the corruption of empire is illegal: that's "democracy," Iraq-style.

Not a Model

What's more, Iraqi Kurdistan has been touted as an island of relative peace and prosperity, ripe for Western investment, and a source of all that "good news" that's supposedly being suppressed by the mainstream media. A massive propaganda campaign—engineered by the GOP [Grand Old Party]-connected public relations firm of Russo, Marsh, and Rogers (RM&R)—has been launched to portray Barzani-land as a model of Iraqi "democracy." According to RM&R:

> Of all the different groups in Iraq that have a vision for the future, the vision of the Kurds is closest to ours. It's important to recognize that the Kurds are not hostile to the West." In addition, "their vision, belief system, and values—they've had a democratic system in place for a while—parallel ours." No doubt, it's "a very messy situation over there and the country is trying to figure out its future. The Kurds would like the rest of country to look at the Kurdish region and see it as a model for the rest of the country.

Yes, the Kurdish gangster state resembles ours in that our rulers and their cronies shamelessly use the state for their own profit: in both cases, the system is based on bribery and corruption, the only difference being that, in the U.S., we still have something we call the rule of law, although the [President George W.] Bush administration has done everything possible to undermine it. In America, it is still possible to collar at least some of these kleptocrats [corrupt officials] and bring them to justice. In Kurdistan, however, and throughout Iraq, there is no law—only party militias on the rampage, offing their opponents and wilding in the streets, even going so far as to kill American journalists who expose their crimes.

We aren't exporting democracy at gunpoint—we're imposing the same sort of corruption that infects Washington, except that, over in Iraq, the kleptocrats are not only above the law, they also have the power to clap anyone who denounces them in jail. And it is the U.S. government that has empowered them. Qadir makes this point in his article entitled "The Winner and Loser in Iraq's New Constitution." He avers that the Iraqi constitution—written under the conditions of occupation and incipient civil war—and the civil order it created were necessarily deformed at birth and rendered illegitimate because

> The overthrow of the former Iraqi regime did not occur by Iraqi hands; and that the foreign forces, which had achieved the regime overthrow under the banner of "Liberation of Iraq" from tyranny and oppression, became itself forces of occupation which does not differ in its behavior, practices, and actions to any other force of occupation in history. Thus, the democratic process which was subsequently forced upon [Iraq by] the forces [of] occupation, carries non-Iraqi fingerprints that increase the doubt amongst the Iraqis to the true impetus behind this process.

A Kleptocracy

Qadir's critique of the Kurdish kleptocracy is particularly sharp on the question of Iraqi "federalism," which he believes is being used as a cover for massive corruption. While acknowledging that the federalist impulse is an expression of the Kurdish desire for self-determination, Qadir points a finger at the Kurdish leadership, writing that they "are not without selfish conflicts and [their] own interests," which are being pursued under the banner of "federalism." "The Kurdish leadership," he writes, "and in particular the leadership of the two main parties, have tired of the sweet taste of power alone" and are now enjoying the "economic privileges" conferred on them by the American victory:

> [Their] power and privileges cannot be maintained without a federalist Kurdish entity which cannot be scrutinized by the federal government of Baghdad. On the other hand, as a sovereign state, the Iraq state will guarantee the Kurdish leadership protestation [Raimondo's note: I think he means protection] from the interferences by the neighboring countries which will prohibit any move towards the establishment of a fully sovereign Kurdish state in the future. In addition, Iraqi Kurdistan has great wealth in natural resource, which the Kurdish leadership wishes to convert into its private and personal property. This cannot be achieved unless the current Kurdish Cartels ruled the Kurdish region itself and alone, as is the case at the moment.

The gangster state of Kurdistan is Abramoff-ism in power. Criminal cartels run the state apparatus, doling out rewards and punishments in a system of bribery and kickbacks—and the occasional gangland-style murder. We are, in short, exporting our own system, albeit with none of the legal and constitutional constraints against the more brazen forms of gangsterism.

The Kurds and the War Party

The effort to dress up the Kurdish tyranny is just one of the more cynical efforts by the War Party [those who supported the 2003 Iraqi invasion] to prettify an abominable abortion as the birth of "democracy" in Iraq. It's no coincidence that RM&R was instrumental in the founding of "Move America Forward," the neocon [conservative faction supportive of intervention abroad] front group running television ads proclaiming the "news" that WMD [weapons of mass destruction] *have* been found in Iraq but the "mainstream media" is suppressing it. In the Bizarro World parallel universe of the War Party, up is down, the president's own admission that the "intelligence" was wrong is discounted, and Kurdistan is a "democratic" utopia "parallel" to ours—where someone can get 30 years in prison for exposing official corruption.

U.S. government officials have promised members of Dr. Qadir's family to investigate his case and report back in two weeks: in the meantime, reports from Amnesty International that he is being tortured—combined with the record of the U.S. military's cooperation with the torturers—is hardly reassuring. The KRG's "Minister of Human Rights," Ihsan Nuri, confirms our worst fears, reportedly telling Awaz Sayd Qadir—the sister of Dr. Qadir—that her brother must "rot and die in jail." In addition, one has to wonder how much pressure the U.S. will bring to bear on their Kurdish clients over the fate of a prominent critic of the American occupation.

Note

1. Jack Abramoff was a lobbyist involved in extensive corruption in the US Congress.

Turkish Actions Against Kurds Constitute Genocide

Rebwar Fatah

In the following viewpoint, a Kurdish writer and journalist says that Turks are committed to eliminating all ethnicities other than Turkish within Turkey. He claims that the Turks have labeled Kurds as terrorists in order to justify the use of force and repression against the Kurdish population. He contends that the Turkish campaign against the Kurds is similar to the genocidal campaign of Saddam Hussein in Iraq and that the Turks are guilty of cultural, linguistic, and physical genocide against the Kurdish peoples. He concludes by providing a timeline of Turkish atrocities. Rebwar Fatah runs the Kurdish news and commentary site KurdishMedia.com.

Since the Armenian genocide, Turkey has done very well to hide and disguise its dark history from the international community. But a shady past rarely dawns a bright future.

Kurds Labeled Terrorists

Instead, Turkey is re-branding itself with Europe-friendly terms to essentially get rid of what it has always wanted to be rid of. Turkey's tidy up of its language: words with a distinct Kurdish

Kurds rallied in support of autonomy and against Turkish oppression during the 2008 spring festival of Nowruz, in Istanbul. © AP Images.

origin wiped out and replaced. Indeed, anything that is not strictly Turkish has been linked to "terrorism"—a trigger word guaranteed to win the sympathies of the international community.

The Turkish constitution does not recognise Kurds in Turkey, and so often labels them as terrorists, providing a convenient scapegoat for military uprisings and other political issues. Thus, "terrorist" becomes a synonym for Kurds.

Turkey frequently argues that the PKK [Kurdistan Workers' Party] is a terrorist organisation; hence all Kurdish organisations are banned for what they may imply.[1]

Turkey is desperately in need of an imaginary threat to its "national security", "territorial integrity" and "sovereignty", achieved by "separatist/terrorist" Kurds. The scale of the suffering Kurds and destruction of Kurdish homeland does not fit into any "terrorist" definition. In 1999, the death toll of Kurds killed in Turkish military operations increased to over 40,000. According to the figures published by Turkey's own Parliament, 6,000 Kurdish villages were systematically evacuated of all inhabitants and 3,000,000 Kurds have been displaced. This sounds like an elimination of a people, a culture and a homeland.

If Turkey is genuine in its elimination of terrorism, it must take brave steps, accepting Kurdish people and their homeland, Kurdistan, and ending its history of oppression.

Professor Noam Chomsky called the Turkish response to Kurds an "ethnic cleansing", resulting in the death of thousands, the emigration of over two million people and the destruction of approximately 6,000 villages.

Turkey Is Like Saddam

In fact, these methods by which Turkey has sought to oppress the Kurdish people are similar to those used by Saddam Hussein in the recent past, including the destruction of Kurdish land, mass evacuation and deportation. In some other areas, Turkey has used more oppressive methods to achieve its "Final Solution" of the Kurdish Issue. Some have found this unsurprising, given Turkey's Ottoman ancestry. During World War I, for example, the Ottoman Empire allied itself with Germany, and in the conflict's immediate aftermath conducted a programme aiming to exterminate the Armenians, Greeks, Yezidis and Alwis. To date, however, Turkey denies these genocidal campaigns.

The oppression of Kurdish people within Turkey can be defined as genocide in various ways; cultural, linguistic and physical all play a part in the cleansing of Kurdish ethnicity from Turkey itself, and are still embraced by the Turkish constitution.

The head of the British Parliamentary Human Rights Commission, Lord Avebury, said of Turkish atrocities in 1996 that,

> Just as many people in western Europe turned a blind eye to Hitler's preparations for the Holocaust in the thirties, the democratic world ignores the evidence of incipient genocide against the Kurds in Turkey today.

As history has shown in Iraq, Turkey cannot attempt to solve the Kurdistan issue with violence and oppression; the days have well passed in which campaigns of genocide can be "success-fully" conducted, and Turkey must look to the future, realising that modern Kurds are not as Kurds from the dark ages.

Examples of Turkish Atrocities

The history of Turks from Ottoman Empire to the Turkish State is a continuous attempt to eliminate any ethnic and religious group that come in contact with them. . . .

1915, April—Organized arrests of a large number of Armenian intellectuals and prominent national leaders in Constantinople and the provinces. They are deported to Anatolia and are killed on the way. The Armenian soldiers of the Turkish army are disarmed and massacred by the thousands. The Armenian population is exiled to the Syrian Desert and massacred. . . .

1920—30,000 Armenians are massacred in the areas of Kars and Alexandropole by Kemalists [followers of Kemal Atafürk, the first president of Turkey].

1920, September—Kemalist Turkey attacks Armenia. The Armenians fight against the Turkish army, but finally they succumb on the 2nd of December 1920. The Turkish victory is followed by a massacre of the Armenians and the annexation of one half of Armenia's Independent Republic of May 28, 1918, to Turkey.

1920 to 1921—Another 50,000 Armenians are executed by Kemalists. . . .

1924, July 10—The Turkish army suppresses the Kurdish revolt in Hakkari. After 79 days, 36 villages are vandalized and destroyed, and 12 others are erased.

1925, February—30,000 Kurds are killed during a revolt against the Turkish authorities. It is estimated that the Kurds have suffered the loss of 500,000 people by massacres and displacements by the Turks over the years.

1925, March 3—The great Kurdish revolution bursts out at Elazig under [Kurdish leader] Seyh-Sait. 10,000 Kurds seize

Harput and attack Diyarbakir, the Capital of Kurdistan after the complete destruction of 48 villages. . . .

1927, May 30—2,000 Kurdish fighters are killed in Amed (Diyarbakir) and Agri. For many days, the waters of the Murat river are turned red by blood.

1937, May 23—The Turkish government forbids the edition of the newspaper of Constantinople "Son Telegraph", because it has referred to the Kurdish sufferings.

1937–1938—The Dersim Genocide. Approximately 40,000–70,000 of Kurdish Alawi (also known as Kizilbash) were killed and thousands were taken into exile. The Dersim Genocide was both continuation of the Kizilbash extermination of the Ottoman times and also an extermination of an ethnically distinct and separate people from Turks. . . .

1978, December 25—Turkish fascists massacre hundreds of Kurds in Marash.

1978, December 28—Proclamation of Martial Law in 15 provinces of Northern Kurdistan prohibiting for years any information about the suffering of the Kurdish people.

1978, December—110 Kurds are massacred in the Northern Kurdistan city of Kahramanmaras.

1979, December to 1980, September—Conflicts between the PKK and the Turkish state provided a distinctively ethnic source of violence. Few thousands Kurds were killed (mostly civilians) in different incidents. . . .

1992, January to 1993, October—Turkish bombing of Kurdish villages. 4,800 are injured, among which 2,000 eventually perish.

1994, May to August—Renewed Turkish raids on Kurds claim the lives of 400 Kurdish villagers and injure more than 200. . . .

1995, March 20—35,000 Turkish soldiers enter Southern Kurdistan under the pretext of fighting the PKK groups that, according to Ankara, had taken refuge there. Through indiscriminate bombing, torture and forced marches on PKK minefields, 200 Kurds are killed, most of whom were non-combatants. More

Armenian Genocide

In April 1915 the Ottoman government embarked upon policies designed to bring about the wholesale reduction of its civilian Armenian population. The persecutions continued with varying intensity until 1923 when the Ottoman Empire itself went out of existence and was replaced by the Republic of Turkey.

The Armenian population of the Ottoman state was reported at a little over two million in 1914. Nearly a million had already perished by 1918, while hundreds of thousands had become homeless and stateless refugees. By 1923 virtually the entire Armenian population of Anatolian Turkey had disappeared and total losses had reached up to 1.5 million. . . .

World War I provided cover for the implemention of the plan to eliminate the Armenian population putatively from the flank of the Ottoman Empire exposed to Russia. The military debacle on the Russian front in December 1914 and January 1915, and the barricading of the Armenian population inside its quarter of the city of Van in April 1915, in fear of threatened massacre, provided a pretext to validate charges of sedition by Armenians and justification for their evacuation. The announced . . . policy aside, the facts of the matter proceeded by a different course. The Armenian population in the war zone along the Russian front was in the main slaughtered in situ [in place] and not subjected to deportation. The mass expulsion of the Armenian population stretched the entire length of the Anatolian Peninsula from Samsun and Trebizond in the north to Adana and Urfa in the south, from Bursa in the west and all other

than 50,000 Turkish troops moved into Southern Kurdistan. Along four routes, a 335 kilometres long border was breached and eyewitnesses noted that advanced Turkish teams were sent some 40 kilometres inside South Kurdistan. Civilian Kurds have been killed and refugee camps have been bombarded from the air. . . .

1999—The death toll of Kurds killed in Turkish military operations rises to over 40,000 and according to the figures pub-

communities around the Sea of Marmara, including the European sector of Turkey, all the way to Erzerum and Harput in the east and everywhere in between, including Ankara, Konya, Sivas, and Malatia.

The beginning of the deportations actually represents the second phase of the annihilation plan. On 24 April 1915 two hundred prominent Armenian leaders in Istanbul were summarily arrested, exiled, and subsequently executed. The expulsions had been preceded since February 1915 by the disarming of Armenian draftees in the Ottoman army, who were then reassigned to labor battalions and were eventually executed. With the elimination of able-bodied men from the Armenian population, the deportation of the civilian population proceeded with little resistance.

The journey of the convoys of families on the open road for hundreds of miles from all across Anatolia toward Syria, through the primary concentration point of Aleppo, resulted in massive loss of human life. The deliberate exhaustion of the population through deprivation of access to water proved a particularly excruciating and effective means of reducing numbers quickly. Though guarded to prevent escape, the convoys were by no means protected. Their arrival at predetermined locations in remote areas turned out to be appointments with the killer units known as the Teshkilati Mahsusa. . . . These wholesale massacres were also occasions for the abduction of children and younger women. In places like Sivas, Harput, and Bitlis, massacres as much as deportation announced the implemention of the policy of genocide.

Rouben P. Adalian, "Armenian Genocide,"
Encyclopedia of the Modern Middle East and North
Africa, ed. Philip Matar, 2nd ed., vol. 1. New York:
Macmillan Reference, USA, 2004, pp. 292–296.

lished by Turkey's own parliament, 6,000 Kurdish villages were systematically evacuated of all inhabitants and 3,000,000 Kurds have been displaced.

Note

1. The PKK engages in armed attacks to destabilize the Turkish government.

Turkey Has Not Mistreated the Kurds

Dan Burton

In the following viewpoint, an American politician argues that the Kurdish revolutionary organization the PKK (Kurdistan Workers' Party) is a Marxist-Leninist terrorist group that often commits violence against Kurdish civilians. He says that Turkey has the right and the duty to fight the PKK and to prevent the establishment of a Kurdish independent state that would destabilize the region. He contends Turkey is a democracy that does not discriminate against or mistreat the Kurdish minority. He concludes that Turkey is a strong regional ally, and that the United States should support Turkey in its fight against terrorism. Dan Burton is a Republican from Indiana in the US House of Representatives.

Mr. Speaker [the speaker of the House of Representatives], there has been much discussion about the future of democracy in Turkey. In a March 14, 1994, *Washington Times* editorial, Turkey's Ambassador to the United States points out that Turkey's fight against the terrorist PKK [Kurdistan Workers' Party] should not be viewed as a threat to democracy. The

Marxist-Leninist[1] PKK has murdered thousands of civilians, many of whom are Kurds who were unwilling to support their terrorist agenda, in an effort to carve a Kurdish state out of the sovereign territory of Turkey.

The PKK Is a Terrorist Organization

I also believe that it is important not to confuse Kurds who have been oppressed under the rule of Saddam Hussein in Iraq and those who reside in Turkey. As Ambassador Nuzhet Kandemir explains in his editorial, "Turkish citizens of Kurdish origin live throughout Turkey and participate without discrimination in all walks of life." "Kurds have served as presidents and prime ministers of the Republic of Turkey" and currently, "they serve in large numbers in Parliament," he adds. While it is natural to be sympathetic to the plight of Kurds in Iraq, I must emphasize that the terrorist activities of the PKK do not have the support of the great majority of Turkish citizens of Kurdish origin.

For those Members of Congress who want a realistic picture of PKK terrorism in Turkey, and who want to know about some of the positive steps which Turkey has taken to benefit its citizens of Kurdish origin, I highly recommend Ambassador Kandemir's editorial [See the *Washington Times*, March 14, 1994, "Turkey Has a Right to Protect Its Democracy," by Nuzhet Kandemir].

Recent press commentary, such as Sen. Dennis DeConcini's (Op-Ed, March 8), has expressed anxiety about the future of democracy in Turkey. Democracy has been a rare, precious and often fragile institution throughout human history, so attentive concern for its preservation is always in order. But it is not correct to view Turkey's fight against terrorist criminals as a sign of democracy in danger. On the contrary, true danger would be signified if a democratic government were unwilling or unable to protect its country's territorial integrity or its citizen's human rights from the depredations of a terrorist organization.

A much-misconstrued event has prompted some of the current concerns: The vote of the General Assembly of the Turkish

Parliament on March 2 and 3 [1994] to lift the immunity of eight Turkish parliamentarians. The vote, taken pursuant to the legal process prescribed in the republic's constitution, occurred in connection with judicial investigations of charges that the eight individuals have engaged in activities against the country's constitutional democratic system and its territorial integrity. The issue is not the political views the parliamentarians have been expressing. None of the individuals have been arrested and none has been stripped of membership in the Parliament. The action regarding their immunity is consistent in principle with the immunity provisions of the U.S. Constitution (Article 1, sections 3 and 6).

No Discrimination Against Kurds

The Turkish constitution provides that all citizens have the same political rights and civil liberties which they may exercise equally, without impediment, regardless of ethnic or religious background. Allegations that the immunities of the eight parliamentarians were lifted because of their pro-Kurdish politics are completely unfounded. Turkish citizens of Kurdish origin live throughout Turkey and participate without discrimination in all walks of life; this is a crucial fact that is widely and wildly misunderstood. Kurds have served as presidents and prime minister of the Republic of Turkey. They serve in large numbers in Parliament, belonging to a wide range of political parties. They enjoy full political representation, and all Turkish citizens, including the great majority of citizens of Kurdish origin, do not support Kurdish extremism.

Such extremism manifests itself most virulently in the violence perpetrated by the PKK, an antidemocratic, indeed Marxist-Leninist, terrorist organization. The violence aims at carving a Kurdish state out of the sovereign territory of Turkey, thereby undermining the peace and stability of the entire region. Since its inception in 1984, the PKK has based its operations on intimidation and extortion. After the Gulf War [in 1990–1991, when

Women hold a poster of modern Turkey's founder, Kemal Ataturk, surrounded by photos of soldiers killed by Kurdish rebels at a protest in Turkey in 2007. The banner reads, "Turks and Kurds are brothers. The PKK is treacherous." © AP Images.

the United States fought Iraq], the PKK increased its atrocities and intensified its attacks on the human rights of Turkish citizens of Kurdish and non-Kurdish origin. It has killed thousands of civilians, many of whom are Kurds whom the PKK claims to serve and represent. The PKK took full advantage of the post-war power vacuum in the areas of Iraq bordering Southeast Turkey, which became a breeding ground for terror. The U.N. Human Rights Commission, in its March 2 resolution, recognized that terrorist organizations perpetrate grievous human rights violations. It condemned such violations and asked its members to cooperate to fight terrorism, as required in a large number of international agreements and resolutions, including those of the Conference on Security and Cooperation in Europe (CSCE) and NATO [North Atlantic Treaty Organization].

Turkey Moving Toward Reform

The Turkish government has accelerated its reform programs for the southeast region. These programs—economic, social and political—have been severely hampered by PKK terror. But the government, operating within the rule of law, is determined to eradicate terror and to continue its reform programs for the region. Economic and social programs claim nearly 17.5 percent of Turkey's total investment capital for enormous development projects in the Southeast, such as the Southeastern Anatolia Project (GAP). GAP alone consumes the equivalent of $1.7 million daily (at 1992 exchange rates). Turkey invests in the southeast 13 times more than it collects in taxes from the region. In 1993, investment there was 1.6 times greater than investment in the Western regions.

Despite the challenges, democracy in Turkey remains strong. The Turkish democratic system is the foundation for existing open, secular, pluralistic society and an expanding free market economy. Since the republic's establishment, the Turkish people and their successive governments have dedicated themselves to furthering these values.

Supporting a strong democratic Turkey in a generally volatile region has long been recognized as an important interest of the United States. For over half a century, Turkey has been a staunch ally of the United States and NATO. In the evolving new world order after the collapse of Soviet communism [in 1991], U.S.-Turkish bilateral relations are a major force for good in a vast region stretching from Central Asia through the Middle East to the Balkans. Turkey's heightened strategic importance at the epicenter of important geopolitical changes increases its potential to expand and deepen its "enhanced partnership" with the United States. Military and economic assistance to Turkey should be evaluated with respect to NATO requirements as an investment in bolstering Turkish democracy.

Turkey's local elections on March 27 [1994] will be conducted according to law, as appropriate for an open, free and democratic society, notwithstanding any attempts by terrorist organizations to poison the country's political climate. We are vigilant and have the wisdom not to play into the hands of those who would undermine Turkish democracy or damage Turkey's deep-rooted relations with its democratic friends and allies in the United States.

Note

1. Karl Marx was a German philosopher who advocated communism and workers' revolution. Vladimir Lenin was a Russian Marxist who led a Communist revolution to found the Soviet Union.

The Kurdish Language and Culture Are Still Under Threat in Turkey

Minhaj Akreyi

The author of the following viewpoint writes that Turkey has long banned the writing of Kurdish. He notes that it was only in 1991 that Kurds were allowed to speak, but not write, Kurdish. He claims that Turkey's banning of Kurdish is against the Charter of the United Nations. He argues that Turkey has allowed Kurds some limited rights only because of pressure from the European Union and that Turkey is not really a democracy as long as it oppresses the Kurds. He concludes that Turkey has no intention of substantially changing its policy of oppressing the Kurds and destroying their culture. Minhaj Akreyi is a writer for many Kurdish news sites.

Kurdish language has been banned in Turkey since the creation of its modern borders in 1923. The Kurds were not allowed to speak their mother tongue, not even in their own homes, in the streets, in any social gatherings, let alone in schools, governmental institutions, or any other places. In fact, according to the Turkish government, the Kurds were non-existent in Turkey and were known as "mountain Turks." The reason behind such denial and censorship was that speaking in Kurdish was a matter of national security, and thus will divide Turkey.

Linguistic Genocide

It was not until January 1991, 72 years after the creation of Turkey, that the Turkish government made a huge—huge in Turkey, or else very minor in humanistic level—concession and allowed "the Kurds, concentrated in 13 provinces, to speak—but not write—their language." However, still, the Kurds were not able to read, write, or study in Kurdish; neither were they allowed to wear their traditional Kurdish clothes; nor were there allowed to be publications of any newspapers, books, magazines, or any other form of writing and there were not allowed to be radios and TVs in the Kurdish language.

Lawmakers hold Kurdish-language newspapers in the Turkish parliament in Ankara. There is growing pressure from Kurdish politicians to allow their language to be used in public settings. © AP Images.

The Kurdish Language in Iran, Turkey, and Iraq

Kurdish is an Indo-European language of the Iranian type. Despite this affinity, and despite the supremacy of Persian which is the only language in which teaching is allowed in Iran, the Kurdish language and literature have retained their originality, have developed and have contributed to the consolidation of national feeling. This development surged forward particularly during the short life of the independent Kurdish Mahabad Republic in 1945–46. Kurdish has been banned in Iran since the 1940s. In the interim, the Kurds of Iran have drawn upon the publications of the Kurds of Iraq, where the Kurdish language and literature have progressed enormously since the Revolution of 1958.

Unfortunately, there has been practically no exchange of literature between the Kurds of Turkey and those of Iran, since the alphabets used in the schools of these two countries are quite different. In Iran all teaching is in Persian, which is written in Arabic script; in Turkey all teaching is in Turkish, which uses the Roman alphabet. . . . The situation is quite different, however, when it comes to the exchange of Kurdish publications between the Kurds of Iran and Iraq; both countries teach the Arabic alphabet and, furthermore, most Kurds in Iran and Iraq speak Sorani, the dialect of Southern Kurdistan.

A.R. Ghassemlou, "Kurdistan in Iran," A People Without a Country: The Kurds and Kurdistan, edited by Gerard Chaliand, rev. ed. New York: Olive Branch Press, 1993, p. 98.

The Kurds make up 17–25 percent of Turkey's population located mainly in southeast Turkey. Since 1923, and with some changes in 1991, the policy on the Kurdish language had remained as brutal, oppressive, assimilative, and a linguistic genocide. When in 2003 Recep Erdogan became prime minister [of

Turkey], he complained that nothing had been changed since the jailing of Kurdistan Workers' Party's leader, Abdullah Ocalan, to increase the rights of the Kurdish language and people.

The Kurdish politicians and activists have long been pushing for reformation in the Turkish policy to allow the Kurdish language to be taught in public educational institutions. The Kurdish political party in Turkey, Peace and Democracy Party (BDP) gathered one million signatures demanding public education to be taught in Kurdish for the Kurds in their region and presented the petition to Parliament's Petition's Commission last week, and was rejected.

Turkey Is Not a Democracy

Turkey, the "only democracy" in the Middle East, has long been breaking the very basic principle of democracy and still is. How can Turkey call itself democratic while depriving 20 million of its citizens the freedom to learn education in their mother tongue? The very identity of any ethnicity comes from their language and once the language is erased or extinct, the ethnicity will become extinct as well. Turkey's policy is not only against the foundation of democracy, but also is against the United Nations Charter:

> Any deliberate act committed with intent to destroy the language, religion or culture of a national, racial or religious group on grounds of national or racial origin or religious belief, such as (1) Prohibiting the use of the language of the group in daily intercourse or in schools, or the printing and circulation of publications in the language of the group; and (2) Destroying or preventing the use of libraries, museums, schools, historical monuments, places of worship or other cultural institutions and objects of the group.

Turkey's hypocrisy is mesmerizing. During his visit to Germany on March 4th, 2011, Turkey's prime minister Recep Erdogan told the 10,000 of Turkish descent in Dusseldorf: "Yes, integrate yourselves into German society but don't assimilate yourselves; no one has the right to deprive us of our culture and our identity." Yet, in regarding the Kurdish education in Turkey, he says: "... But do not request education in the mother tongue from us because the official language of Turkey is Turkish." What about the Kurdish culture and identity, Mr. Prime Minister? What gives you and the Turkish government the right to deprive us of our most basic and fundamental right?

It is only evident that Turkey has no intention of being democratic and giving the Kurdish people their natural right of learning education in their mother tongue; and it is only evident that their reasoning of no longer banning the Kurdish language to be spoken in private in 1991 was due to pressure from European Union and not on humane principles. It is also evident from the rejection of the petition last week to teach Kurdish in public education. Turkey should learn from the philosophy of Nelson Mandela [the South African leader and human rights advocate]—whom in 1999 received Turkey's highest award, the Ataturk International Peace Prize, which initially he refused on the basis of human rights violation against the Kurds—which he beautifully professes: "if you talk to a man in a language he understands, that goes to his head. If you talk to him in his mother tongue language, that goes to his or her heart."

CHAPTER 3

Personal Narratives

Chapter Exercises

1. ## Writing Prompt

   Imagine that you were a Kurdish child at the massacre in the village of Gizi. Write a one-page diary entry describing the events of the massacre and your reaction to them.

2. ## Group Activity

   Form groups and develop five interview questions to ask Turkish Kurds about their relationship to their culture and their experiences in trying to preserve it.

A Kurd Who Grew Up in Turkey Laments the Denial of His Cultural Identity

Edip Yuksel

In the following viewpoint, an intellectual figure in the Islamic reform movement discusses his experiences as a Kurd living in Turkey for the first decades of his life. He reports that his brother was killed as a young man by racist Turkish bullies, and that he was imprisoned and tortured by the Turkish government. He argues that the West must stop providing arms and support to the Turkish government, which systematically oppresses the Kurds. He also remembers how as a young boy his father banned the speaking of Kurdish in their home, causing great hardship to his mother. He contends his father had little choice but to conform to widespread Turkish prejudice and pressure against Kurdish. Edip Yuksel teaches philosophy and logic at Pima Community College.

As an individual I have many components. I can define myself in many ways depending on the context. I am a homo sapien, a monotheist, Yahya's and Matine's father, a husband, a Turkish author, a philosopher, a lawyer, a skeptic, a believer, a democrat, a conservative, an American, a political activist, a reformist, a chess-player, a copywriter, a poet, a handyman, a

Edip Yuksel, "Yes, I Am a Kurd," *Journal of International Law and Practice*, Fall 1998.

Macintosh user, a teacher, . . . and I am also a Kurd. I am not sure how being a Kurd ranks among the manifold ingredients that make up my personality, but recently it became one of the important characteristics. Why? Because I have realized that I am denied of this identity. I have also witnessed that many others who share the same culture and heritage are oppressed and killed just because of being born in a Kurdish family.

I Am a Kurd

I am a Kurd who is less articulate in his mother tongue compared to the other four languages that I have learned, namely, Turkish, Arabic, Persian and English. I am a Kurd who lost his 21 years-old brother 19 years ago in Istanbul to the racist bullets of Gray Wolves or Turkish Nationalist militants. I am a Kurd who was put in the same prison, for writing on religious-political issues, with the murderers of his brother and almost lost his life to the knives and teeth of Nationalist Gray Wolves! I am a Kurd who was systematically tortured in Turkish prisons [Yuksel was sentenced to six years in Turkish prisons because he published two articles advocating Islamic revolution in Turkey] because of refusing to recite the Turkish Anthem that contains lines, such as, "I have lived free since eternity; which psychopath dare to chain me." I am a Kurd who was compelled to chant "Happy is he who can call himself a Turk" and declare that "A Turk is worth the entire universe" throughout elementary, middle and high-school years. I am a Kurd whose Kurdish father prohibited the Kurdish language at home in order to survive in a city where being Kurd was regarded as being ignorant and lower class. I am a Kurd who now enjoys eating rice with a fork, unlike Kurds who prefer a spoon. I am a Kurd who wrote scores of books in Turkish and English, but none in Kurdish.

Alas, I was almost blind to the plight of my people until I immigrated to United States and studied law in my late thirties. At age 40, after a wife, two children and citizenship in the United States, I started reading about the history of my people, their tribal system, their innocence, ignorance, wisdom, heroism, betrayals, blunders, dialects, culture, poverty, mythologies, religions, mountains, rebellions, genocide, atrocities, and their current ordeal in a rugged land dominated by four ruthless and racist countries: Turkey, Iraq, Iran, and Syria.

My People Are Denied

The pictures of Kurdish children, men and women whose faces rarely show a smile now talk to me; I cannot escape their questioning eyes: brayi Edip [brother Edip], you managed to become a best-seller author in Turkey, you managed to escape to America, the land of freedom, you managed to get a doctorate degree in law, you write and talk about God, about freedom and human rights, but how can you ignore us?

If you look at their eyes carefully they will talk to you too: you the civilized people, you the citizens of the Western civilization, how can you ignore us? How can you donate arms to the racist Turkish government who is committed to exterminate us? How can you stand by when thousands of us were suffocated to death, our babies in our hands, by the chemicals provided by your corporations? How can you talk about morality, human rights, civilization while we are subjected to systematic genocide by your current or former allies?

My people are denied their identity, their culture, language, naming their own children, using their own land and living in freedom and security.

You might have paid money to watch the [1997] movie *Titanic* and cried for the fate of the passengers who tragically drowned in cold waters 84 years ago. There are people on this planet who are being deliberately subjected to tragedies in their everyday life. Kurds are slaughtered and massacred by the bombs, jets and helicopters made in the U.S. and given by the U.S. As a proud citizen of the civilized world, how can you cry for the people who were drowned 84 years ago, but do nothing while your tax money is spent to support the racist Turkish genocide against the Kurdish population in the South East Turkey?

Forgive me for these bitter words. I am the worst bystander, since I could use my pen when it was much sharper and younger to speak for those who can only speak with lines of sadness on their faces, lost limbs and graves of massacred and assassinated relatives. . . .

I Miss My Mother Tongue

After reading several articles on the linguistic, social and political aspects of bilingualism, certain memories of my childhood revived with much more meaning. Those articles did not contain much new information. They were common sense for me, since I had experienced most of the cases. However, I did not have a clear and systematic interpretation of my experiences. Now I know the reason my father suddenly forbid us from speaking Kurdish after we moved to the city. Now I realize how oppressive the government was. Now I appreciate the importance of bilingual education.

I was raised in a bilingual family. I spoke Kurdish until I was eight years old. At age nine, when we moved from a small eastern town to Istanbul, the biggest city in western Turkey, I was suddenly obliged to speak Turkish. Turkish was the only national language with high prestige. Indeed, it was the only prestigious language of my country. Kurdish, the language of approximately . . . twelve million, had much negative connotation. Speaking Kurdish was a declaration of ignorance and inferiority. Though at that age I was not fully aware of this racist attitude, I was influenced. My father did not have enough ammunition to fight against that pressure. He could not protect our original self-esteem. He submitted fully, even in the privacy of his home. Fighting back probably would be useless. The city with its mighty social, political and economical institutions was a ruthless mold reshaping every irregular individual thrown in. In order to resist that terrible molding machine you needed to be economically independent and heroically resistant. Unfortunately, my father was neither.

We were molded.

The communication language of our family changed dramatically. My father declared martial law against his own mother language which he had spoken until his late forties. My mother did not know a single Turkish word when we were banned from speaking our mother language. It was not that difficult for my father. He had learned Turkish as his fourth language while doing his military service. He had studied Arabic and Persian in religious schools. Being one of the top experts in Arabic language, he was invited to teach Arabic at the university. While he was trying very hard to polish his Turkish, we were struggling to communicate with our mother; sometimes sneaking in Kurdish.

In retrospect, I see that our family was victimized by the ruling majority. As a result, I traded my Kurdish for Turkish. My father ended up teaching Arabic in Turkish with a heavy Kurdish accent. My poor mother started speaking a new language, Kuturkish, a mishmash of Kurdish and Turkish. Nobody could understand her except us. Curiously, I started missing my mother tongue. I hope I will be able to recover it in its pure form. Alas, I am not sure whether my mother will be able to understand it.

A Kurdish Politician Gives Personal Impressions of Saddam Hussein

Sami Abdul-Rahman, interviewed by **Frontline**

In the following viewpoint, an interview with the Public Broadcasting Service television show Frontline, *a longtime Iraqi Kurdish activist discusses his personal impressions of Saddam Hussein. He says that Hussein originally appeared to be charming and intelligent, but that this first impression concealed a very complicated and cruel personality. He contends that Hussein was most likely responsible for an assassination attempt in 1971 on the leader of the Kurdish Democratic Party (KDP), Mustafa Barzani. Sami Abdul-Rahman was a leader in the KDP and held the post of deputy prime minister of the Kurdish Regional Government from 1999 to 2004, when he was killed in a suicide bombing.*

Frontline: *Can you remember the first time you met Saddam Hussein and what your personal impressions were at that time?*

Sami Abdul-Rahman: When first time I met him it was 1970. I had already heard that he is a rising strong man in the Ba'ath Party and the government. And that he wants to solve the Kurdish problem. He was a smart elegant young man, who talked very logically and in strong but friendly terms. So the impression all of us got about him was a very positive impression.

Indeed it was the most positive impression compared with all the other members of the Ba'ath leadership.

Not a Straightforward Person

Describe what he was like personally.

He would study the person who wanted to meet him. He would try to know beforehand what this person is visiting him for. And he would meet them in very proper way. Politely also. But also, always showing an aura of power and strength. But with no arrogance. And, as I said, he would study what are the requests to be made in this meeting? And sometimes he would make the offers before the request was mentioned. Which of course would delight the person who has come for the interview.

The impression people have of him today is of an educated thug. But what you're describing is somebody who is also intelligent, clever, a good tactician and politician. How do you reconcile the different images of Saddam?

If somebody wants to take Saddam just as a simple and straightforward person, he would make a wrong judgment. He is not only a double personality, he has several personalities. In one respect he can be very polite, he can be very nice. But certainly he is very very cruel, and crimes done against the Kurdish people and the rest of the Iraqi people under his regime are unlike any other time in Iraqi history—which has generally been unfortunately a bloody history.

After the 1970 agreement—in which you were part of the negotiating team with the Kurds—you entered the Iraqi government as part of that agreement. At the time Saddam was vice president. What was your impression of his power at that time?

When the Ba'ath came to power, 1968, to my knowledge he first took three things into his hands. The security forces. The media. He couldn't take the army, obviously, he was a young civilian. But he controlled the Ba'ath Committee in the army. And certainly he has also his hand on the finances to spend on these instruments.

This was his first act of taking power. In 1970 when we made the agreement, he was a rising star in the Ba'ath Party but there were other strong men. Within a year and a half he removed every possible rival. So only [General Ahmed Hassan al-]Bakr was left, the president.

And he tried to kill General [Mustafa] Barzani, your leader. How was it possible for you to continue serving in the Iraqi government after that?

You are talking about the attempt on General Barzani's life on the 29th of September 1971. The team certainly was sent by the Baghdad security. And we in the leadership thought the man behind it was Saddam Hussein.

So, after . . . I told General Barzani I think it's very inappropriate that we go on working in a Government that has been trying to assassinate our leader. He told me privately, 'if you leave the Government there will be fighting soon. Who is with us?' And also he said publicly, I don't want to stop negotiations. . . .

But this sad event was the end of confidence in the Ba'ath regime and in Saddam Hussein specifically. And from then on everybody I think knew, at least the KDP [Kurdish Democratic Party] leadership knew, that an attack from the central government would come whether sooner or later, or rather sooner. And both sides began to look for friends and allies and I think that was the prerequisite that prepared the ground for the relationship between Mustafa Barzani and the United States.

Kurdish Survivors Remember Saddam Hussein's Gas Attacks

Wendell Steavenson

In the following viewpoint, written on the eve of the 2003 US invasion of Iraq, a journalist interviews Iraqi Kurds who survived Saddam Hussein's 1988 attack on the city of Halabja. That assault included chemical gas attacks. The survivors describe the panic in the city and the horror of losing loved ones. The author reports that those exposed to the chemicals continue to have babies with birth defects. Survivors of Halabja criticize the United States for using Halabja as an excuse for the 2003 invasion while doing nothing in 1988. However, survivors hope that the US invasion may reduce violence in Kurdistan. Wendell Steavenson has written for American and British publications including Time, *the* Telegraph, *and* Prospect; *she is the author of* The Weight of a Mustard Seed *about Iraqi general Kamel Sachet.*

Haifa Akhmed, a young Kurdish mother, looked down yesterday at her baby girl—born just hours before. "Many Kurds give their children names like Awara, which means displaced," she said, "but I am thinking of the name Nouria, which means love, faithfulness."

A mass grave holds most of the victims of the March 1988 chemical attacks on Halabja, Iraq. Seventy-five percent of the five thousand people killed during the attacks were civilian women and children. © 2004 Getty Images.

Kurds Are Alive

The baby was born 15 years to the day after the infamous Iraqi chemical attack on the Kurdish town of Halabja which killed 5,000 people, almost all of them civilians.

Haifa said she was 11 years old in 1988, and remembers her brother being injured by shrapnel. "The sadness of the day can't be described," she said. "I am from Halabja and I want to compensate for the 5,000 people who were killed then, and to prove that Kurds are alive."

With war looming again [as the United States plans to invade Iraq] the anniversary came at a poignant moment. President George W Bush drew attention to the atrocity in a radio address at the weekend. But as survivors marked the anniversary yesterday some also recalled how the West was backing Iraq at the time and all but turned a blind eye to the atrocity as Baghdad's enemy, Iran, was still seen as the greater threat.

"If America is using this attack on Halabja as a justification for war, then they should have attacked Saddam [Hussein] in 1988, not now," said Rubar Mohammad, 32, who lost a husband she suspects is buried in one of Halabja's mass graves.

"It is too late to raise this issue now. It should have been talked about when it actually happened."

Rubar was speaking in Sulaimaniya, a city in northern Iraq some 45 miles north-west of Halabja. It was not until 1991 that Kurds went back into Halabja after managing to liberate it.

Almost every family in Halabja lost someone in the chemical attack, the worst ever against civilians. Jabar Abdullah has collected shell casings used in the attack and displays them in the middle of the road every anniversary as a memorial.

He remembers 3,000 people trying to find shelter in the tobacco processing plant, at six storeys, the highest building in the town.

"I lost three cousins," he said. "People were vomiting, some were blind, some had blistered skin. It was a day when a father couldn't help his own son, when mothers left behind their children. People were driving their cars over bodies to save themselves."

Three of Akhmed Hussein's sons died on the way to the Iranian border. His wife later died from chemical exposure in a Teheran hospital.

Remembering the flight from Halabja, he said: "I couldn't concentrate, my head was circling. We just became calm and couldn't speak. One son had his head on my leg and was sleeping when he died; we didn't even notice."

Chemical Effects Linger

The survivors of Halabja fled to Iran, returning to their ruined and deserted homes only after the Kurdish uprising of 1991, which eventually took control of Kurdistan from Saddam's Iraqi regime.

Much of the town has been rebuilt with UN help, but the legacy of the attack continues.

Haifa's baby was born healthy but according to Dr Shinow Hussein Abdullah there is an increased incidence of miscarriage and abnormal births in Halabja. Some babies have malformed skulls and exposed brains and cannot survive more than a few minutes. Others have spinal cysts that leave them disabled.

"The parents are normal and have no problems," she said, "but then they explain that they were here during the chemical attack."

Halabja has tried to recover but the situation remains insecure. In the hills above the town, Ansar al-Islam, some 800 Islamist Kurds augmented by itinerant Arab jihadis, nightly shell the environs and Kurdish *peshmerga* [fighters] positions opposing them. People are injured and sometimes killed.

Rija Mohammed has designed a memorial to the attack—a large open hand surrounded by 16 missiles, to mark the date as the 16th and three narcissus flowers to symbolise March.

He remains hopeful that an American war will drive Saddam out and Ansar with him. But he is uncertain. "I am sure the Americans are taking care of their own interests more than those of humanity.

"Halabja should be a message to those countries that sold Saddam Hussein his chemicals: chemical bombs should never again be used against civilians."

A Kurdish Writer Remembers His Time in Saddam Hussein's Prisons

Jalal Barzanji

In the following viewpoint, a Kurdish poet and writer who grew up in Iraq describes being imprisoned for his writings by Saddam Hussein's regime from 1986 to 1989. He says that after hearing the stories of other Kurdish prisoners, he knew his arrest and torture were imminent. Still, he says, when he was actually arrested one evening and taken away while still in his pajamas, it was a shock. He describes the filthy and brutal conditions of his cell, including poor food and no clothing except the pajamas he arrived in. He also describes being subjected to repeated sessions of torture. Jalal Barzanji now lives in Canada.

Handcuffed and blindfolded, I was dragged away and kicked and punched and finally thrown onto a hard surface. A door was shut, and I could no longer hear my mother's and other prisoners' soulful cries. I could tell I was back in a military vehicle. As the vehicle started moving, the biggest worry in my heart was the image of the young people shot in front of me and my mother: how she was going to take it and what might they do to her?

Jalal Barzanji, "A Deathly Quiet Cell," *The Man in Blue Pyjamas: Prison Memoir in the Form of a Novel*. Edmonton: University of Alberta Press, 2011, pp. 14–24. Copyright © 2011 by University of Alberta Press. All rights reserved. Reproduced by permission.

Anticipating Torture

I had no idea where we were heading. I was rolling about in the back the vehicle and a blow to my head nearly knocked me out. Why was I still handcuffed and blindfolded? This was surely to torment my soul, I said to myself. But I wasn't going to let them do to my soul what they had done to my body. They could confuse me about my whereabouts, but they couldn't break me down. I couldn't escape, I knew, but my soul couldn't be conquered.

I was in the midst [of] these thoughts when suddenly they removed the blindfold. Perhaps they wanted to make me see something horrific again, I thought, so I kept my eyes shut. But when I opened my eyes, I was in a van with two secret policemen standing over me. They must have been the ones kicking and punching me. As though to confirm this, one of the men kicked me really hard in the chest, calling me many names.

I returned the insults.

Enraged, the other guy kicked me so hard that I fell on my back and nearly fainted. I had no energy to sit or stand, but I was conscious enough to look through the van's rear window and through the window on the driver's side. The hue of the sky told me that it wasn't night yet.

As we drove, I forced my mind to think of other things. I recalled the road where students would work on their homework by the roadside because they did not have room in their own homes. In my junior year (Grade 11), I had been one of those children by the roadside.

When the vehicle stopped, I was blindfolded again. In my mind, I was trying to prepare myself for the long haul, thinking that perhaps I would be languishing in prison for years to come without trial, without ever being allowed to see a lawyer. Perhaps I would die under torture. But I didn't entirely rule out the power of bribery. A hefty bribe, I thought, was all that was needed to put an end to my misery.

Even before my arrest, it was very hard for me not to think about what it would be like to be imprisoned in the secret police headquarters. On my drive south along the main thoroughfare through Hawler, I could see the police headquarters, and my mind involuntarily tried to get behind those walls. How did the prisoners manage under torture? How did they pass the time? What it was like to be kept in isolation and in the dark? Just pondering such questions would make me feel like a prisoner already, although even without such thoughts it was very hard not to feel imprisoned. People were being watched everywhere, and even if they weren't it didn't matter because people felt spied upon regardless, even in their bedrooms.

Every so often, my friends and I would go for a walk, which would usually culminate in a visit to the civil servants' club in the evening. Located in the city centre, the club's sprawling rose garden, surrounded by huge eucalyptus trees, was an ideal place for drinks and a conversation about the arts and literature. In winter, the inside of the club, with its floor-to-ceiling windows, offered an even better refuge from the ever-present ears of Saddam [Hussein]'s regime. The civil servants' club was where teachers went to discuss their classes, but when the government took it over it became a garage. Later still, after the collapse of Saddam's regime [in 2003, after the U.S.-led invasion], it became Nishtimani Mall. Part of this new mall was built on a large old cemetery, called Sheikh Allah Cemetery. I don't know whether the reason for the mall's unsuccessful sales had to do with the fact that it was the first mall in Hawler, or the fact that it was built on top of a cemetery in which some of the loved ones of the shoppers were laid to rest.

My Turn Would Come

Sometimes we would meet at an old tea house called Majko, which was located in the heart of the old city. Every evening, writers from the city would go there to see each other, drink tea, and discuss various topics. Since Majko was more intimate than the club, it was easier for us to vent our frustrations against the military dictatorship, even though there was nothing we could do to change the situation. Getting together like this was indeed a big relief for all of us, even though it made us more aware of how little freedom we had. Talking about freedom was like talking about something that we could never get or find. We were aware that life could not be enjoyed without freedom and that without freedom truth was impossible. We knew our freedom had been taken away from us, but it wasn't until I became a prisoner that I began to realize how horrific life behind bars was. Nothing had prepared me for the cruelty of being taken away from my wife and child.

Somehow I had always known my turn would come. You see, Saddam's regime was not the type that would be satisfied with leaving literary types like me alone. The regime wanted to take over everybody. I wanted to have an independent existence, but the regime wouldn't allow it. That's why I knew it was only a matter of time. Still, it was quite a shock when they came for me that chilly evening. I was planning on taking a much-needed bath and then going to bed. It was hard to believe I was being led away like that, blindfolded and handcuffed with nothing on but my flimsy blue pyjamas.

Since I was blindfolded most of the time I was in the vehicle, I was unable to keep track of time. But my mind was active: one moment, I would seriously believe my mind was capable of transforming the prison into an island of freedom and tranquility; another moment, however, I would become desperate and consider myself a fool.

What was happening to me was not something new or different. It had happened before to others. And it would happen again. Saddam would imprison people and then release them. Before their release, the prisoners would be given a pep talk about their responsibilities and how much harsher their penalties would be if they returned to their old ways. They would be told they would be kept under constant surveillance. The aim was to keep the people in a constant state of paranoia. Saddam did not invent the art of imprisonment and torture; he merely perfected it. That's why after their release many would try to find a way to seek asylum overseas. But that wasn't easy. Ordinary Iraqis were not allowed to have passports. The only way to leave was to be smuggled through difficult and dangerous terrain, a practice that over the years claimed many lives.

A year before my arrest, a man in our neighbourhood called Safeen was one of those prisoners Saddam released. As was customary in our culture, people went in droves to visit him when he came out of prison. Listening to Safeen tell his story made me wonder if I could endure what he had endured. He was hung from a ceiling fan and beaten daily with a thick cable. His fingernails and toenails were pulled out. Cigarettes had been stubbed on his chest, and he had been made to sit naked on a bottle. Lying there in the back of the vehicle, I tried to tell myself that I would be all right, but inside I wasn't so sure.

In the Cell

I was trying not to mind my pains when the vehicle suddenly stopped. I was blindfolded once again and punched twice so severely that I fell. I was kicked repeatedly until my body became numb. I was like a punching and kicking bag for these men. I was alert enough to wonder why they had so much anger towards me; they had never seen me before. I blamed their cruelty on the dictatorship. They were, after all, men trained to be cruel by the regime.

I was dragged out of the vehicle and pushed with such force that I fell onto the ground and bruised my head. Then they picked me up and dumped me into a very narrow room, so narrow in fact that I couldn't stretch my legs or arms. With the blindfold and handcuffs removed, I now saw that I was sitting on a dirty old blanket on a concrete floor. I was still wearing my blue pyjamas. I checked to see if I was bleeding. A drop or two fell on the pyjamas, and I wiped off the rest with my sleeve. The drops of blood left a big stain.

It was very cold. I remember wondering why I had changed so fast the previous evening. If I had remained in my black pants and grey coat I would not have been so cold. When I moved the blanket a little, I saw traces of blood and hardened human waste all over the floor. I tried to think of things beyond this tiny room. Nice things, like Fridays.

Friday was the most anticipated day of the week when we were young. On that day, everyone cooked a delicious meal. My father would chop the head off a chicken in front of the house. I used to be happy that the chicken was being killed in a moral way, but I could never stand to watch and always closed my eyes so that I didn't have to see the blood. Now my own fresh blood mixed with the dried blood of other prisoners who had been here before me. My entire body hurt. I worried a lot about my mother, how devastating it would be for her to see me so weak and bloody in this, the second prison I had been held in since my arrest. I thought of what Safeen had told me and realized, given all the moaning and crying I was suddenly hearing, what lay head.

A yellow light burned constantly in the cell. The switch was outside the door where I could not reach it, so I could not tell whether it was day or night. Suddenly the tiny iron window above the cell door was opened from outside and a small loaf of old bread and a bottle of water were thrown down. With the place being so small, they landed on my lap. The cap of the bottle opened from the impact and half of the water spilled out. It was warm and smelly; the bottle had been filled and refilled with tap water. Even though I had not been given any food until now, I had no desire to eat. When I tried to stretch my right foot a little, I revealed some markings and dates and numbers that previous prisoners had left on the wall. What was most startling to me was that these people had used their own blood to leave traces of themselves behind. Perhaps this was their way of trying to lessen their pain and remind themselves that the cruelty they had been subjected to could not go on forever. But somehow the idea of using blood as a means of communication revolted me. My forehead was still bleeding lightly, but I just couldn't bring myself to write with the blood.

From 1979 until 1991, Amna Suraka was a secret prison where the Ba'ath regime interrogated, tortured, and killed Kurdish prisoners. It is now a museum, and its displays include statues depicting how prisoners where tortured. © soran hamawandi/Demotix/Demotix/Corbis.

Torture

I was still reflecting on what was on the wall when suddenly the door was flung open and two men with powerful shoulders and arms dragged me out, handcuffed and blindfolded me once again, and led me away, kicking me repeatedly from behind. A few minutes later, they ordered me in Arabic to stop, removed the blindfold, and made me sit on the bare floor. All around me were tools of torture: on a steel desk there were cables, bottles, pliers, and hammers; electric wires were snaking out of the wall; a black rope was dangling from the ceiling, under which was a chair. I wondered how many innocent throats had been strangled in that room.

Safeen's words were painfully vivid in my mind, and I realized that I was here to be tortured. They undressed me with such a force that they nearly tore up my pyjamas and the shirt I was wearing. At least they let me keep my underwear on. Then they turned on me with the cables. Everything became dark before my eyes, and I started to faint, but somehow I remembered what my friend Abd had told me about the way his father had described the fires of Jahanam. I wondered which was worse, being in Hell or being here. I remember, vaguely, at one point they were lifting me up to where the ceiling fan was. I must've fainted completely shortly afterwards, for when I regained consciousness I was back in my cell. I could hear the loud cries coming from other prisoners being tortured. I was blue and black all over now. My knees hurt the most, and I was feeling a little cold, but as I was too weak to put my pyjamas back on, I wrapped myself in the dirty old blanket.

As a child, I had hurt my knees playing soccer. Back then, my mother helped me clean my wounds and soothe the pain with home remedies so that I was able to sleep that night. There was no one to soothe my injuries this time. But the biggest annoyance was the strong ceiling light, which was constantly on. It made my wounds burn painfully, and it kept me permanently disoriented. In the midst of all this, thinking about writing and about more pleasant memories gave me a glimmer of hope.

My torturers were two men. I couldn't tell whether it was morning or evening, day or night, when they came for me, but it seemed to be every other day. One of them had a face full of pimples and a small tattoo in the shape of a dot perched on the tip of his nose. His thick moustache seemed to have been dyed jet black in the fashion of the times, but I think his heart must have been blacker. They never got tired of torturing me; they treated my body as though it was a carcass.

But it was the guy with the pimples who did most of the torturing. He would start with the cable, and after several blows he would shout, "Now admit your guilt. Who are these people who write against our revolution?" I always said the same thing, that I was a poet and that I was only writing about human desire, peace, and beauty. Then the beating then would continue. Afterwards I would be as good as dead. Back in my cell, I would slowly return to consciousness.

One day, I heard someone tapping on the wall, and when the tapping continued, I realized it was from the adjacent cell. I never discovered who was in that cell, but through tapping we kept in touch and made our concern for one another known. It was a small thing, I know, but tapping made us feel connected.

Interrogation

I had been left alone in my cell for what I thought was several days when one morning two different men came for me. I tried to put my torn blue pyjamas on, but they dragged me out before I could do so. Once they had taken me out of my cell they blindfolded me, wrapped the old blanket around me, and shoved me away to what felt like another part of the prison compound. When they removed the blindfold, I found myself face-to-face with an officer dressed in an olive uniform. His desk was cluttered with papers.

He fired off questions and comments in a business-like way: "How many poems have you written under a pseudonym attacking our great revolution? We know you write for underground publications. We know that your brother, Kamal, instead of turning himself in, fled to the mountains. Obviously, he has something to hide."

The news about Kamal caught me by surprise. At the time of my arrest, my younger brother was finishing high school at an evening school. That evening, Kamal had arrived at school as usual. His English teacher, Ali Jukil, pulled him aside and told him that the secret police had come looking for him. At once Kamal grabbed his books and fled to the Setaqan neighbourhood where one of our relatives, Bawakir's son, arranged his escape to the village of Senan in the Smaquli Valley southeast of Hawler. There he stayed for a while with my aunt and her husband, Sayyid Salih, and then joined the *peshmerga* [Kurdish rebels].

The officer continued: "Let me make it clear to you: you can spare yourself further trouble by coming clean. All you need to do is to tell us who these people are who attack our revolution in *Shakh*, the subversive underground magazine. They publish this in the mountains, so how do they get submissions from people here in the city?"

I had indeed written a few pieces in the 1980s under the pseudonym Zamand for the then underground *The Kurdistan Writer*, the organ of the Kurdistan Writers' Union. But since they didn't mention this, I decided they probably didn't know about it. But what if they had the publication right there in the drawer? I told him that the information they had on me was not accurate and added, "And as for my brother, Kamal, well, I'm a prisoner. How could I know his whereabouts? I am a family man. He's only twenty years old; he doesn't live with us. He's responsible for himself; I'm responsible for myself."

The officer who interrogated me told me to shut up and said that I was not in prison to argue or give explanations. I had been arrested only to admit my crime.

Only, I had committed no crime.

The officer was not happy with what I had to say. He said they would get everything out of me by force. I was blindfolded yet again and taken back to my cell. On the way I was kicked repeatedly; twice I came close to slipping on the stairway. I had a feeling they knew I was innocent, but that it mattered little to them. I was afraid I would die under torture and that my family would be forever kept in the dark about it.

My friend Safeen was released on Saddam's birthday after doing five years, and what he'd told me about his experiences gave me some clue about what lay ahead for me. If I could bear the torture for a few months, I might turn out to be all right. Sentenced to die without a trial was of course a possibility. Ending up languishing in Abu Ghraib or Badush, two of Saddam's most notorious prisons, for years to come was another. I hadn't done anything wrong and I was determined to tell them that the next time they took me for interrogation. I also wanted to tell them again that as a poet I only wrote about peace, love, and beauty.

I knew I had lost some weight because my pyjamas were very loose. I also was covered in rashes. I was desperate for a bath and for some good food. Imagine nothing else but bread and water every day. I had cramps in my stomach and was constantly constipated. But to be denied pen and paper was simply beyond endurance. I wanted a complete record of my imprisonment, but I was afraid I couldn't rely entirely on memory. Pen and paper would've been my salvation.

Glossary

Anfal campaign A genocidal campaign against the Kurds and other non-Arab peoples by the Iraqi regime of Saddam Hussein from 1986 to 1989. It included poison gas attacks on Kurdish populations.

Armenian genocide The systematic killing of the Armenian population in the Ottoman Empire (later Turkey) during and just after World War I. Some Kurds participated in attacks on the Armenians.

Ba'ath Party An Arab nationalist political party. It was the political party of Saddam Hussein, the longtime ruler of Iraq.

Gulf War A 1990–1991 war between a US-led coalition and Iraq in response to Iraq's invasion of Kuwait.

Iran-Iraq War A war between Iran and Iraq from 1980 to 1988. It was inspired by territorial disputes and sectarian conflict between Iran's Shia religious rulers and Iraq's secular Sunni government.

Iraq War A 2003–2011 war between a US-led coalition and Iraq ostensibly to rid Iraq of weapons of mass destruction.

Kurdistan The region in which Kurds form the majority of the population. It roughly includes eastern Turkey, northern Iraq, northwestern Iran, and northern Syria.

PKK The Kurdistan Workers' Party, a Kurdish revolutionary socialist organization that has been fighting an armed struggle against the Turkish state for an autonomous Kurdistan since 1984. It is listed as a terrorist group by many states and organizations, including the United States.

Shia The second-largest denomination of Islam in the world. Iran and Iraq are both Shia majority countries; Shia Muslims form an important minority in Turkey. Some Kurds are Shia Muslims.

Sunni The largest denomination of Islam. Sunni Muslims are a majority in Turkey and an important minority in Iraq and Iran. The government of Saddam Hussein in Iraq was predominantly Sunni. Many Kurds are Sunni Muslims.

Organizations to Contact

The editors have compiled the following list of organizations concerned with the issues debated in this book. The descriptions are derived from materials provided by the organizations. All have publications or information available for interested readers. The list was compiled on the date of publication of the present volume; the information provided here may change. Be aware that many organizations take several weeks or longer to respond to inquiries, so allow as much time as possible.

Amnesty International
5 Penn Plaza, 14th Floor
New York, NY 10001
(212) 807-8400 • fax: (212) 463-9193
e-mail: aimember@aiusa.org
website: www.amnestyusa.org

Amnesty International is a worldwide movement of people who campaign for internationally recognized human rights. Its vision is of a world in which every person enjoys all of the human rights enshrined in the Universal Declaration of Human Rights and other international human rights standards. Each year it publishes a report on its work and its concerns throughout the world. Amnesty International's website includes numerous reports and news items about the status of the Kurds.

Carnegie Endowment for International Peace (CEIP)
1779 Massachusetts Ave., NW
Washington, DC 20036
(202) 483-7600 • fax: (202) 483-1840
e-mail: info@ceip.org
website: www.ceip.org

This private, nonprofit organization is dedicated to advancing cooperation between nations and promoting active international engagement by the United States. It publishes the quarterly journal *Foreign Policy*, a magazine of international politics and economics that is published in several languages and reaches readers in more than 120 countries. Its website includes numerous news articles and publications, including "The Turkish Constitution and the Kurdish Question" and "The Future of Kirkuk."

Human Rights Watch
350 Fifth Ave., 34th floor
New York, NY 10118-3299
(212) 290-4700 • fax: (212) 736-1300
e-mail: hrwnyc@hrw.org
website: www.hrw.org

Founded in 1978, this nongovernmental organization conducts systematic investigations of human rights abuses in countries around the world. It publishes many books and reports on specific countries and issues as well as annual reports, and other articles. Its website includes numerous discussions of human rights and international justice issues as they relate to the Kurds.

Institute for the Study of Genocide (ISG)
John Jay College of Criminal Justice
899 Tenth Ave., Room 325
New York, NY 10019
e-mail: info@ instituteforthestudyofgenocide.org
website: www.instituteforthestudyofgenocide.org

The ISG is an independent nonprofit organization that exists to promote and disseminate scholarship and policy analyses on the causes, consequences, and prevention of genocide. To advance these ends, it publishes a semiannual newsletter and working papers and holds periodic conferences; maintains liaison with academic, human rights, and refugee organizations; provides consultation to representatives of media, governmental, and nongovernmental organizations; and advocates passage of legislation and administrative measures related to genocide and gross violations of human rights. In addition to newsletters, the ISG publishes books on the topic of genocide such as *Ever Again? Evaluating the United Nations Genocide Convention on Its 50th Anniversary and Proposals to Activate the Convention.*

International Criminal Court (ICC)
PO Box 19519, 2500 CM
The Hague, The Netherlands
+31 (0)70 515 8515 • fax: +31 (0)70 515 8555
e-mail: visit@icc-cpi.int
website: www.icc-cpi.int/Menus/ICC/Home

The ICC is a treaty-based international court established to try the perpetrators of the most serious crimes of concern to the international community. Its website includes annual reports on the activities of the court, information about situations and cases, relevant legal texts, and other information.

Iraq Foundation
1012 14th Street, NW, Suite 1110
Washington, DC 20005
(202) 347-4662 • fax: (202) 452-7897
e-mail: iraq@iraqfoundation.org
website: www.iraqfoundation.org

The Iraq Foundation is a nonprofit organization working for democracy and human rights in Iraq, and for a better international understanding of Iraq's potential as a contributor to political stability and economic progress in the Middle East. The foundation was established in 1991 by Iraqi expatriates with the purpose of working with Iraqis and non-Iraqis in promoting its vision. It publishes a newsletter (available on its website). Its website also includes news items and discussions of its projects and humanitarian work.

Kurdish Institute of Paris
06, rue La Fayette, F-75010
Paris, France
+33 (0)1 48 24 64 64 • fax: +33 (0)1 48 24 64 66
website: www.institutkurde.org/en/institute

The Kurdish Institute is an independent, nonpolitical organization devoted to Kurdish culture and making the general public aware of the Kurdish situation. It publishes numerous periodicals and books, mostly in Kurdish, as well as recordings of Kurdish music and videos, including *The Voice of Kurdistan*, a documentary tracking the principal events of Kurdish history.

Montreal Institute for Genocide and Human Rights Studies (MIGS)
Concordia University
1455 De Maisonneuve Blvd. West
Montreal, Quebec, H3G 1M8 Canada
(514) 848-2424, ext. 5729 or 2404 • fax: (514) 848-4538
website: http://migs.concordia.ca

MIGS, founded in 1986, monitors native-language media for early warning signs of genocide in countries deemed to be at risk of mass atrocities. The institute houses the Will to Intervene (W2I) Project, a research initiative focused on the prevention of genocide and other mass atrocity crimes. The institute also collects and disseminates research on the historical origins of mass killings and provides comprehensive links to this and other research materials on its website. The site also provides numerous links to other websites focused on genocide and related issues, as well as specialized sites organized by nation, region, or case.

Prevent Genocide International (PGI)
1804 S Street, NW
Washington, DC 20009
(202) 483-1948 • fax: (202) 328-0627
e-mail: info@preventgenocide.org
website: www.preventgenocide.org

PGI is a global education and action network established in 1998 with the purpose of bringing about the elimination of the crime of genocide. In an effort to promote education on the subject of genocide, PGI maintains a multilingual website both for the education of the international community, as well as for the nations not yet belonging to the United Nations Genocide Convention in an effort to persuade these countries. The website maintains a database of government documents and news releases, as well as original content provided by members.

STAND/United to End Genocide
1025 Connecticut Ave., Suite 310
Washington, DC 20036
(202) 556-2100
e-mail: info@standnow.org
website: www.standnow.org

STAND is the student-led division of United to End Genocide (formerly Genocide Intervention Network). STAND envisions a world in which the global community is willing and able to protect civilians from genocide and mass atrocities. In order to empower individuals and communities with the tools to prevent and stop genocide, STAND recommends activities from engaging government representatives to hosting fund-raisers, and has more than a thousand student chapters at colleges and high schools. While maintaining many documents online regarding genocide, STAND provides a plan to promote action as well as education.

United Human Rights Council (UHRC)
104 N. Belmont Street, Suite 313
Glendale, CA 91206
(818) 507-1933
website: www.unitedhumanrights.org

The UHRC is a committee of the Armenian Youth Federation. By means of action on a grassroots level, the UHRC works toward exposing and correcting human rights violations of governments worldwide. The UHRC campaigns against violators in an effort to generate awareness through boycotts, community outreach, and education. The UHRC website focuses on the genocides of the twentieth century.

US Department of State
2201 C Street, NW
Washington, DC 20520
(202) 647-4000
website: www.state.gov

The US Department of State is the agency of the federal government responsible for foreign affairs. Its website includes daily press briefings, reports on policy issues, and numerous other articles. The site includes fact sheets and other information about Iraq, Turkey, Iran, as well as many articles about the Kurds.

List of Primary Source Documents

The editors have compiled the following list of documents that either broadly address genocide and persecution or more narrowly focus on the topic of this volume. The full text of these documents is available from multiple sources in print and online.

Constitution of the Iraqi Kurdistan Region, April 19, 2004

The constitution of the semiautonomous Kurdish region established de facto following the US invasion of Iraq.

Constitution of Turkey, November 7, 1982

The governing document of Turkey. Critics claim it denies fundamental rights to Kurds by not recognizing Kurds as an ethnic group in Turkey. Others deny there is any discrimination in the constitution.

Convention Against Torture and Other Cruel, Inhuman, or Degrading Punishment, United Nations, 1974

A draft resolution adopted by the United Nations General Assembly in 1974 opposing any nation's use of torture, unusually harsh punishment, and unfair imprisonment.

Convention on the Prevention and Punishment of the Crime of Genocide, December 9, 1948

A resolution of the United Nations General Assembly that defines genocide in legal terms and advises participating countries to prevent and punish actions of genocide in war and peacetime.

Principles of International Law Recognized in the Charter of the Nuremburg Tribunal, United Nations International Law Commission, 1950

After World War II (1939–1945), the victorious allies legally tried surviving leaders of Nazi Germany in the German city of Nuremburg. The proceedings established standards for international law that were affirmed by the United Nations and by later court tests. Among other standards, national leaders can be held responsible for crimes against humanity, which might include "murder, extermination, deportation, enslavement, and other inhuman acts."

Recommendations of the European Commission on Turkey's Progress Towards Accession to the European Union, October 6, 2004

Official recommendations by the European Union on Turkey's application to join the European Union. The recommendations include discussions of Turkey's policy towards the Kurds.

Remarks by US President Barack Obama to the Turkish Parliament, April 6, 2009

US president Barack Obama discusses Turkish-American relations, including Turkish progress on Kurdish rights and the conflict with the Kurdistan Workers' Party (PKK).

Rome Statute of the International Criminal Court, July 17, 1998

The treaty that established the International Criminal Court. It establishes the court's functions, jurisdiction, and structure.

United Nations General Assembly Resolution 96 on the Crime of Genocide, December 11, 1946

A resolution of the United Nations General Assembly that affirms that genocide is a crime under international law.

United Nations Security Council Resolution 1441, November 8, 2002

A resolution adopted by the UN security council offering Iraq under Saddam Hussein a final opportunity to comply with its disarmament obligations. It provided the grounds for the US-led invasion of Iraq.

Universal Declaration of Human Rights, United Nations, 1948

Soon after its founding, the United Nations approved this general statement of individual rights it hoped would apply to citizens of all nations.

US Congressional Iraq Liberation Act of 1998

A bill passed by both houses of Congress that states the case for overthrowing Saddam Hussein. Saddam's crimes against the Kurds are listed and discussed.

Whitaker Report on Genocide, 1985

This report addresses the question of the prevention and punishment of the crime of genocide. It calls for the establishment of an international criminal court and a system of universal jurisdiction to ensure that genocide is punished.

For Further Research

Books

Gerard Chaliand, ed., *A People Without a Country: The Kurds and Kurdistan*, trans. Michael Pallis. Northampton, MA: Interlink, 1993.

Quil Lawrence, *Invisible Nation: How the Kurds' Quest for Statehood Is Shaping Iraq and the Middle East*. New York: Walker & Company, 2008.

Aliza Marcus, *Blood and Belief: The PKK and the Kurdish Fight for Independence*. New York: New York University Press, 2007.

David McDowall, *A Modern History of the Kurds*. 3rd ed. New York: St. Martin's Press, 2004.

Kevin McKiernan, *The Kurds: A People in Search of Their Homeland*. New York: St. Martin's Press, 2006.

Susan Meiselas, *Kurdistan: In the Shadow of History*. 2nd ed. Chicago: University of Chicago Press, 2008.

Denise Natali, *The Kurdish Quasi-State: Development and Dependency in Post–Gulf War Iraq*. Syracuse, NY: Syracuse University Press, 2010.

Cenk Saracoglu, *Kurds of Modern Turkey: Migration, Neoliberalism and Exclusion in Turkish Society*. London: Tauris Academic Studies, 2010.

Nicole F. Watts, *Activists in Office: Kurdish Politics and Protest in Turkey*. Seattle: University of Washington Press, 2010.

Kerim Yildiz, *The Kurds in Iraq: The Past, Present and Future*. 2nd ed. Ann Arbor, MI: Pluto Press, 2007.

Periodicals and Internet Sources

Tim Arango, "Iraq's Factional Chaos Threatens to Disrupt a Kurdish Haven," *New York Times*, January 3, 2012. www.nytimes.com.

Mohammed Ayoob, "Turkey's Kurdish Conundrum," *Foreign Policy*, November 9, 2011. http://mideast.foreignpolicy.com.

BBC, "Killing of Iraq Kurds 'Genocide,'" December 23, 2005. http://news.bbc.co.uk.

Max Boot, "The Way of the Kurds," Council on Foreign Relations, May 24, 2010. www.cfr.org.

Stephen Farrell and Baghdad Bureau, "What Iraqis Think of the American Withdrawal: Kurdish Region," *New York Times*, December 17, 2011. http://atwar.blogs.nytimes.com.

Kaya Genç, "Turkey's Kurds Must Push for a Democratic Answer," *Guardian*, August 31, 2011. www.guardian.co.uk.

Gendercide Watch, "Case Study: The Anfal Campaign (Iraqi Kurdistan), 1988," n.d. www.gendercide.org.

Jeffrey Goldberg, "After Iraq," *Atlantic*, January 2008. www.theatlantic.com.

Jürgen Gottschlich, "Kurds Fear New Civil War May Be Brewing," *Der Spiegel*, October 5, 2011. www.spiegel.de.

Michael M. Gunter, "Kurdish Nationalism in the Aftermath of the Arab Spring," *Foreign Policy*, November 8, 2011.

Heval Hylan, "Genocide in Kurdistan," Gendercide Watch, November 2000. www.gendercide.org.

Constanze Letsch, "Mandatory Turkish Puts Kurdish Pupils at Disadvantage," *Guardian*, December 28, 2011. www.guardian.co.uk.

Hoshiar Molod, "Turkey Is Not Far from Committing Kurdish Genocide," *Kurdish Aspect*, February 11, 2008. www.kurdish aspect.com.

Meghan L. O'Sullivan, "Kurds May Lead the Way for the Arab Spring," Council on Foreign Relations, June 16, 2011. www .cfr.org.

Reihan Salam, "A Virtual Kurdistan?," *The Agenda—National Review Online*, June 17, 2011. www.nationalreview.com.

Toros Sarian, "The Kurds and the Armenian Genocide," *Massis Post*, July 28, 2011. http://massispost.com.

Liam Stack, "For Kurds in Turkey, A Country's Conflict Rends Families," *New York Times*, October 29, 2011. www.nytimes .com.

Washington Post, "Who Are the Kurds?," February 1999. www .washingtonpost.com.

Jon Wiener, "Should Israel Arm Kurdish Terrorists?," *The Nation*, September 17, 2011. www.thenation.com.

Allen Yekikan, "The Kurdish Struggle Against Genocide," *Haytoug Magazine*, July 2, 2009. www.haytoug.org.

Websites

Forgotten Genocides Project—Al-Anfal and the Genocide of Iraqi Kurds (www.ncas.rutgers.edu/center-study-genocide -conflict-resolution-and-human-rights/al-anfal-and -genocide-iraqi-kurds-1988). This website is part of an on-line effort by the Rutgers Center for the Study of Genocide, Conflict Resolution, and Human Rights. It focuses on the Iraqi Anfal campaign against the Kurds and includes a summary, maps, photographs, and an extensive bibliography of websites, reports, films, and press reports about the Anfal campaign.

Kurdish Human Rights Project (www.khrp.org). This website includes reports and news pertaining to the Kurdish regions. It also includes background information, photos, and other information.

Shaking Hands with Saddam Hussein (www.gwu.edu/~nsar chiv/NSAEBB/NSAEBB82). This web page examines the United States' friendly relations with Saddam Hussein from 1980 to 1984. It includes a historical background and numerous downloadable diplomatic documents.

Film

In the Name of Honour This 2000 documentary examines the oppression of Kurds in northern Iraq and how violence is being directed more at women.

Index